PORTFOLIO / PENGUIN

EVERY NATION FOR ITSELF

Ian Bremmer is the president of Eurasia Group, the world's leading global political risk research and consulting firm. He has written for *The Wall Street Journal*, *The Washington Post*, *Newsweek*, *Foreign Affairs*, and other publications. His eight books include the international bestseller *The End of the Free Market* and *The J Curve*. He lives in New York City and Washington, D.C.

ALSO BY IAN BREMMER

The End of the Free Market:
Who Wins the War Between States and Corporations?

The Fat Tail: The Power of Political Knowledge
for Strategic Investing (with Preston Keat)

The J Curve: A New Way to Understand
Why Nations Rise and Fall

Managing Strategic Surprise: Lessons from Risk Management
and Risk Assessment (with Paul Bracken and David Gordon)

New States, New Politics:
Building the Post-Soviet Nations (with Raymond Taras)

Nations and Politics in the Soviet
Successor States (with Raymond Taras)

Soviet Nationalities Problems
(with Norman Naimark)

EVERY NATION FOR ITSELF

What Happens When No One
Leads the World

IAN BREMMER

Portfolio / Penguin

to ann and rob (and moose)

PORTFOLIO/PENGUIN

Published by the Penguin Group
Penguin Group (USA) Inc., 375 Hudson Street,
New York, New York 10014, USA

USA | Canada | UK | Ireland | Australia | New Zealand | India | South Africa | China
Penguin Books Ltd, Registered Offices: 80 Strand, London WC2R 0RL, England
For more information about the Penguin Group visit penguin.com

First published in the United States of America by Portfolio/Penguin,
a member of Penguin Group (USA) Inc., 2012
This paperback edition with a new preface published 2013

THE LIBRARY OF CONGRESS HAS CATALOGED THE HARDCOVER EDITION AS FOLLOWS:

Bremmer, Ian, 1969–
Every nation for itself: winners and losers in a G-zero world / Ian Bremmer.
p. cm.
Includes bibliographical references and index.
ISBN 978-1-59184-468-6 (hc.)
ISBN 978-1-59184-620-8 (pbk.)
I. Economic development. 2. International cooperation. 3. World politics. 4. Leadership.
I. Title.
HD82.B6917 2012
330.9—dc23
2011052900

Printed in the United States of America
1 3 5 7 9 10 8 6 4 2

Set in Granjon
Designed by Spring Hoteling

While the author has made every effort to provide accurate telephone numbers, Internet addresses, and other contact information at the time of publication, neither the publisher nor the author assumes any responsibility for errors or for changes that occur after publication. Further, publisher does not have any control over and does not assume any responsibility for author or third-party Web sites or their content.

CONTENTS

CONTENTS

PREFACE

In June 2012, United Nations Secretary-General Ban Ki-moon opened the United Nations Conference on Sustainable Development, also known as the Rio+20 summit, with a warning: This gathering is too big to fail. But for President Barack Obama, British Prime Minister David Cameron, and German Chancellor Angela Merkel, the event was apparently too big to attend.

These leaders understood that, given the wide divergence of interests among policymakers of the world's largest economies and the current inability of any country or group of countries to lead others toward compromise, these meetings were no more likely to produce credible, detailed agreements on sustainable development than the 2009 Copenhagen climate summit, described in the opening pages of this book, was to produce meaningful progress on climate change. Recent meetings of the World Bank and IMF have been better attended, but no more likely to solve pressing global problems.

The 2012 presidential campaign reflected the G-Zero reality.

President Obama talked again about building consensus among U.S. allies to achieve foreign-policy goals, but his first term demonstrated just how hard durable alliances are to build and sustain. His singular foreign-policy achievement, the killing of Osama bin Laden, needed buy-in only from the members of Seal Team 6. Holding together a NATO-led coalition in Afghanistan proved impossible, and Washington remained a spectator throughout most of the Arab Spring.

This is the central foreign-policy concern confronting Barack Obama as he begins his second term as president. Some Americans will continue to refer to the man and the office as "leader of the free world," but the reality, as Obama has already learned, is that no one, not even America's president, has the power in today's world to drive a global agenda.

In fact, since *Every Nation for Itself* was first published last year, the G-Zero phenomenon and resulting lack of global leadership have only intensified—and analysts from conservative political scientist Francis Fukuyama to liberal Nobel Prize–winning economist Joseph Stiglitz have since written of the G-Zero as a fact of international life. The risk of confrontation in Asia has grown—between China and Japan (the world's second- and third-largest economies) in the East China Sea, and between China and several Southeast Asian countries in the South China Sea. The U.S. transition toward a sharper foreign-policy focus on Asia and progress toward a U.S.-led Trans-Pacific Partnership on trade that excludes China has combined with U.S. elections and China's once-a-decade leadership transition to further fuel tensions between Washington and Beijing. Fights over commercial and investment rules, cyber security, and the clash between the state-driven and free-market varieties of capitalism have gathered momentum.

Given its more limited role in a G-Zero world, the United States finds advantage in a multilateral approach to foreign-policy challenges. Washington will try to build its security ties with other countries and deepen its economic integration in Asia with a single massive trade deal, while China uses its economic weight to influence policy within Asian neighbors on an individual basis. Neither approach will create an overwhelming regional advantage, and it will become more difficult over time for Asian states to maintain both close commercial relations with China and tight security ties with America. Japan, in particular, will find itself in a bind.

In the Middle East, Syria's civil war has deepened, with crucial implications for local heavyweights Turkey, Iran, and Saudi Arabia—and even for Russia. Attacks on U.S. diplomatic targets in Libya, Egypt, Yemen, and elsewhere have heightened Washington's aversion to direct involvement in the region's conflicts. Sanctions threaten to destabilize Iran, and sectarian tensions have stoked violence in Iraq. This is another region in which a lack of global leadership fuels rivalries among local actors, and there is little reason to expect that the Middle East's most powerful states can reach the kind of accommodation needed to restore stability anytime soon.

In both Asia and the Middle East, these are competitions without referees.

Who will provide global leadership? U.S. policymakers are fully occupied with domestic questions, particularly those involving efforts to revitalize U.S. economic growth and to address long-term debt problems. Europe also remains distracted. Encouraging signs have appeared in recent months that the Eurozone's crisis of confidence will force European leaders to fix important flaws in the single currency's original design. That's good news for Europe's longer-term future, but the journey along the road from here to there will take time, and a more activist foreign policy will remain a luxury that European policymakers cannot afford.

Nor will major emerging powers look to shoulder new burdens.

The most striking development since the book first hit shelves has been the sharp economic slowdowns in China, India, Brazil, and other major developing markets. It's a useful reminder that there is no guarantee that every emerging power will fully emerge, and the slowdowns in these countries create more than enough domestic headaches to ensure that their governments are even less willing to take on the costs and risks that come with a greater share of global leadership.

The result is that regional leaders—not a single global heavyweight—will probably be left to keep the peace. In Asia, the U.S.-Chinese balance of power will become more crucial. In the Middle East, Turkey, Iran, and Saudi Arabia will compete to shape the region and bolster its stability. Given that both these forms of competition will generate uncertainty, we can expect a continuation of the political and market turmoil that has been building these past four years.

Finally, this volatility also reminds us that when uncertainty is the order of the day, safety becomes a crucial commodity. That's why the United States remains the world's investment safe haven—and why, for better and for worse, not even ratings agency downgrades can make it more difficult for America's government to borrow money—at least for the moment. Over the longer term, Washington will have to address the growing imbalances on U.S. books. But U.S. officials will have the time and space to help reestablish strong growth, even as they make tough decisions that will set a path toward America's future.

Ian Bremmer
New York City
February 15, 2013

INTRODUCTION

G-Zero—*JEE-ZEER-oh*\– *n*
A world order in which no single country or durable alliance of
countries can meet the challenges of global leadership.

One beautiful Napa Valley evening in October 2011, I found myself in conversation with Paul Martin, the man who created the G20—the forum where nineteen countries plus the European Union bargain over solutions to pressing international challenges. I had just given a speech arguing that the G20 is an unworkable institution, liable to create as many problems as it solves.

As Canada's finance minister from 1993 to 2002 and then prime minister from 2003 to 2006, Martin had irked his country's allies by declaring that Western dominance of international financial institutions was on the wane. He argued that the world needed a club that welcomed new members from among the leading emerging powers. Officials in Washington, Western Europe, and Tokyo had politely ignored Martin's idea—until the 2008 financial crisis forced them to admit he might have a point. Three years later, the G20 was a fixture of international politics.

Martin and I began a good-natured debate. I argued, as I had in my speech, that the G20 is more aspiration than organization, that twenty is too many, and that there is too little common ground for substantive progress on important issues except under the most extreme conditions. Martin countered that the G20 gives more countries than ever a stake in the success of the global economy and in resolving the world's political and security challenges.

Then the conversation took an unexpected turn. Martin explained that his early advocacy for the G20 was based less on a vision of global governance than on what was best for Canada. His country had long been a member of the G7—a privileged position, to be sure, but within an increasingly irrelevant organization. By arguing for the acceptance of a trend he considered inevitable, Martin believed that Canada could exchange its first-class seat on a sinking ship for a secure spot on a bigger boat. And by leading the effort to build that boat he also hoped to win his country valuable new friends. Like every other delegation present, Canada had its own reasons for being there.

Later that evening, as I replayed our conversation in my mind, I found myself imagining an enormous poker table where each player guards his stack of chips, watches the nineteen others, and waits for an opportunity to play the hand he has been dealt. This is not a global order, but every nation for itself. And if the G7 no longer matters and the G20 doesn't work, then what is this world we now live in?

* * *

For the first time in seven decades, we live in a world without global leadership. In the United States, endless partisan combat and mounting federal debt have stoked fears that America's best days are done. Across the Atlantic, a debt crisis cripples confidence in Europe, its institutions, and its future. In Japan, recovery from a devastating earthquake, tsunami, and nuclear meltdown has proven far easier than ending more than two decades of political and economic malaise. A generation ago, these were the world's powerhouses. With Canada, they made up the G7, the group of free-market democracies that powered the global economy. Today, they struggle just to find their footing.

Not to worry, say those who herald the "rise of the rest."[1] As established powers sink into late middle age, a new generation of emerging states will create a rising tide that lifts all nations. According to a much-talked-about report published by London-based Standard Chartered Bank in November 2010, the global economy has entered a "new 'super-cycle' driven by the industrialization and urbanization of emerging markets and global trade."[2] New technologies and America's emergence lifted the global economy between 1870 and the onset of World War I. America's leadership, Europe's reconstruction, cheap oil, and the rise of Asian exports drove growth from the end of World War II into the 1970s. And we can count on increasingly dynamic markets in China, India, Brazil, Turkey, and other emerging nations to fuel the world's economic engine for many years to come. Americans and Europeans can take comfort, we're told, that other states will do a larger share of the heavy lifting as our own economic engines rattle forward at a slower pace.

But in a world where so many challenges transcend borders—from the stability of the global economy and climate change to cyberattacks, terrorism, and the security of food and water—the need for international cooperation has never been greater. Cooperation demands leadership. Leaders have the leverage to coordinate multinational responses to transnational problems. They have the wealth and power to persuade governments to take actions they wouldn't otherwise pursue. They pick up the checks that others can't afford and provide services no one else will pay for. On issue after issue, they set the international agenda. These are responsibilities that America is increasingly unwilling, and incapable, of assuming. At the same time, the rising powers aren't yet ready to take up the slack, because their governments must focus on managing the next critical stages of their own economic development.

Nor are we likely to see leadership from global institutions. At the height of the financial crisis in November 2008, political leaders of the world's most influential established and emerging countries gathered in Washington under the banner of the G20. The forum helped limit the damage, but the sense of collective crisis soon lifted, cooperation quickly evaporated, and G20 summits have since produced virtually nothing of substance. Institutions like the UN Security Council, the International Monetary Fund, and the World Bank are unlikely to provide real leadership because they no longer reflect the world's true balance of political and economic power.

If not the West, the rest, or the institutions where they come together, who will lead? The answer is no one—neither the once-dominant G7 nor the unworkable G20. We have entered the G-Zero.

This book is not about the decline of the West. America and Europe have overcome adversity before and are well equipped over the long run to do it again. Nor is this a book about the rise of China and other emerging-market players. Their governments stand on the verge of tremendous tests at home. Not all of them will continue to rise, and it will take longer than most expect for those that emerge to prove their staying power. Rather, this book details a world in tumultuous transition, one that is especially vulnerable to crises that appear suddenly and from unexpected directions. Nature still hates a vacuum, and the G-Zero won't last forever. But over the next decade and perhaps longer, a world without leaders will undermine our ability to keep the peace, to expand opportunity, to reverse the impact of climate change, and to feed growing populations. The effects will be felt in every region of the world— and even in cyberspace.

The pages that follow will define this world and anticipate the turmoil to come. Chapter 1 explains what the G-Zero is. Chapter 2 details how we got here, from the rise of American power and Western-dominated institutions following World War II to the geopolitical and economic upheaval of the past few years. Chapter 3 takes on the G-Zero's impact on the world around us: politics, business, information, communication, security, food, air, and water. Chapter 4 looks at the ability of countries, companies, and institutions to navigate the risks and opportunities created by the G-Zero world—and separates the era's winners from its losers. Chapter 5 asks what comes next, and offers predictions on the international order that grows out of the G-Zero. The sixth and final chapter provides ideas on how Americans can shape—and help lead—that new world.

The world has entered a period of transition and remarkable upheaval. For those who would lead nations and institutions through this volatile moment, the G-Zero will demand more than great power or deep pockets. It will require agility, adaptability, and the skill to manage crises—especially those that come from unexpected directions.

CHAPTER ONE

What Is the G-Zero?

It is better to be alone than in bad company.
—George Washington

On December 17, 2009, Denmark's Queen Margrethe celebrated a much-anticipated climate summit with a gala dinner in Copenhagen's Christiansborg Palace. Leaders and distinguished guests from around the world enjoyed salt cod puree, scallops, dessert, and a musical performance by the Band of the Royal Life Guards. If the queen's "life guards" weren't enough to inadvertently underscore the theme of climate change, the event also included recordings of Frank Sinatra singing "Here's That Rainy Day" and of George Harrison performing "Here Comes the Sun." Queen Margrethe managed to ignore diplomatic niceties that should have seated her next to the evening's longest-serving visiting dignitary—Zimbabwe's President Robert Mugabe, a man better known for brutalizing opponents, stoking racial violence, and gutting his country's economy than for his charming dinner conversation or commitment to reversing global warming. "We know that some people don't want to sit next to others," explained a Danish protocol officer to a reporter. "It's like a family dinner. You don't want Uncle Louis sitting next to Uncle Ernie."[1]

Queen Margrethe's dodge gave the summit its first and only success.

A week after the conference closed, Xinhua, China's state-run news agency, published a story alleging that Chinese premier Wen Jiabao had learned during the dinner that U.S. president Barack Obama had invited friends and allies for a "clandestine" meeting later that evening to discuss negotiating strategy—and that China's delegation had not been included.[2] It remains unclear whether such a meeting was scheduled or if Wen got bad information. It's possible the entire story was concocted by the Chinese government to justify Wen's absence from a key meeting the next day and his delegation's refusal to agree on a final deal. Whatever the truth, Wen withdrew to his suite at the Radisson Blu Hotel—and the summit went nowhere.

Much of what we think we know about the following day's closed-door negotiations comes from a secret recording, two 1.2-gigabyte sound files "created by accident" and obtained by the German newsmagazine *Der Spiegel*.[3] On December 18, two dozen heads of state gathered in the Arne Jacobsen conference room in Copenhagen's Bella Center to hash out differences on a common approach to climate change. More than a hundred other world leaders waited outside the room for the principals to produce an agreement. China's premier remained at the Radisson.

Instead of bargaining with his fellow head of state Wen Jiabao, the president of the United States found himself negotiating with

He Yafei, a Chinese deputy foreign minister well known for his exceptional command of English and his willingness to use it to advance his country's worldview—with sometimes provocative arguments. German chancellor Angela Merkel and French president Nicolas Sarkozy pressed China and India to commit to binding targets on the reduction of greenhouse gas emissions. China and India announced they could not support a document that imposed specific numerical targets, even on the Americans and Europeans. Norwegian prime minister Jens Stoltenberg asked Indian officials how they could renounce the very plan they had proposed just a few hours earlier. President Mohamed Nasheed of the Maldives, an island chain that lies in the Indian Ocean about seven feet above sea level, demanded that the Chinese delegation explain how it could ask his country to "go extinct." Sarkozy accused the Chinese of "hypocrisy," He Yafei lectured the group on environmental damage from the Industrial Revolution, several NGOs accused Western officials of blocking a deal, and a few journalists accused Obama of selling out Europe by letting China off the hook. Not to be ignored, Venezuelan president Hugo Chávez called Obama the devil. A gathering that then–British prime minister Gordon Brown had hyped as "the most important conference since the Second World War" ended in acrimony and conflicting accounts of what had happened, and with no progress toward any meaningful agreement.

But here's the key takeaway: The summit didn't collapse because China was snubbed, India is irresolute, the Europeans are stubborn, or Obama is lord of the underworld. It failed because (a) there was not nearly enough common ground among the leading established and emerging players to reach a deal that would have required sacrifice from all sides, and (b) no single country or bloc of countries had the clout to impose a solution.

This argument perfectly illustrates the G-Zero and where it

comes from. Rising powers like China, India, Brazil, and South Africa claim that 150 years of industrialization in the West have inflicted nearly all the damage that now has climate scientists in a panic. They insist that Americans and Europeans have no right to expect developing countries to sharply limit their growth to clean up the rich world's mess. They have a point. The established powers counter that developing states will do most of the environmental damage in decades to come. They add that climate change is a global problem, one that can't be solved without substantial help from developing countries, even if America and Europe cut emissions to zero. They have a point, too. The urgent issue is that, as with so many of today's political and economic questions, the world needs established and emerging powers to agree to share both benefits and burdens. Doing nothing will make matters much worse.

This is the G-Zero challenge. To prevent conflict, grow the world economy, manage our energy needs, implement farsighted trade and investment policies, counter transnational threats to public health, and meet many other tests, the world needs leaders who are willing and able to shoulder burdens and enforce compromise. To be sure, many countries are now strong enough to *prevent* the international community from taking action, but none has the political and economic muscle to *remake* the status quo. No one is driving the bus.

AMERICA AND THE COST OF LEADERSHIP

America was hardly the first modern nation to use its global power to reinforce international peace and maintain the flow of commerce. England, later Britain, was already one of the world's most formidable naval powers by the beginning of the eighteenth cen-

tury, and the final defeat of Napoleon in 1815 left it in a domin
position for nearly a century. Throughout this period, Britain acte
as the primary provider of global public goods—services that profit
nearly everyone and for which no one wants to pay. For example,
Britain helped keep the peace by working to maintain a balance of
force among the great powers of Europe. It promoted an increasingly open world economy, in part by using its unparalleled naval
power to protect international sea lanes. It enabled capital flows and
maintained the gold standard. The British pound served as the
world's primary reserve currency.

The rise of Germany and the United States in the late nine-
teenth century began to undermine Britain's dominance, and the
breakdown of Europe's concert of nations gave way to the First
World War. But it was World War II that permanently crippled
Britain's ability to continue in this role. The United States, which
suffered much less damage from the two conflicts than its enemies
or its allies, proved ready, willing, and able to take on global leadership. For the next several decades, it did exactly that.

With the end of the Cold War, the United States looked set for
an extended run as the world's sole superpower. Yet, as has become
abundantly clear in recent years, America's debt is on the rise. The
country's increasingly heavy financial burden is not simply a product of George W. Bush–era spending inspired by the multifront
war on terror or of the Obama administration's expansionary response to the financial crisis of 2008–2009. America's debt problem—arguably, its debt crisis—is a slow-motion emergency that
has been developing in plain sight for decades under presidents and
congressional majorities of both parties. In an especially vivid study
on this subject, scholar Michael Mandelbaum has detailed how U.S.
lawmakers balanced the federal budget in just five of the forty-
seven years before financial markets began melting down in the fall

of 2008. Entitlement programs like Social Security (America's pension plan), Medicare (health insurance for the elderly), and Medicaid (health insurance for the poor) have now grown large enough to consume about 40 percent of the U.S. federal budget.

Accelerating the issue, the 77 million American baby boomers born between 1946 and 1964 began to qualify for pension and health benefits in 2011. Once that wave has fully crashed, the total cost will be almost four times the size of the entire 2010 American economy.[4] As pension and health care costs have risen, so have U.S. deficits. Within a generation, Washington will be spending more money servicing the country's debt than it does on defense.

To help finance this debt, the United States now borrows about $4 billion per day, nearly half of that from China. But the Chinese government has fed American fears that it won't continue to bankroll U.S. consumption. Senior Chinese officials have publicly expressed doubts that U.S. debt can remain a sound long-term investment and warn that the demands of ambitious political and economic reforms within China will force Beijing to spend more of its money at home. In 2009, Wen Jiabao admitted, "We have lent a huge amount of money to the U.S. Of course we are concerned about the safety of our assets. To be honest, I am definitely a little worried."[5] The recent debt ceiling crisis only exacerbated Chinese concerns. Said Stephen Roach, chairman of Morgan Stanley Asia, "This is China's wakeup call. . . . They [will] stop buying dollar-based assets, not because they're mad at us . . . but just because they don't need to do it."[6]

To help Washington meet its growing obligations, Americans will have to pay higher taxes, but tax hikes alone won't rebalance the books. Policymakers must cut spending on both entitlements and defense. For tens of millions of workers, retirement will have to wait a little longer, pension and health benefits will be less generous, and the architects of American foreign policy will face tough choices about what Washington can and cannot afford. Without these sacrifices the nation will risk financial disaster on a scale not seen since the 1930s.

American foreign policy faces additional limits. A raft of polls suggests that Americans worry much more about their jobs, their homes, their pensions, and their health care than about the export of American values or even dangers from abroad—a trend that has widened sharply over the past several years.[7] In an age of austerity, Americans have less interest in helping manage turmoil in the Middle East, rivalries in East Asia, or humanitarian crises in Africa, and they insist that elected officials sharpen their focus on domestic challenges. The September 11 terrorist attacks triggered a surge in U.S. public interest in foreign policy, but that was mainly a result of the unprecedented arrival of foreign problems on American soil and the impact of terrorism on confidence in the U.S. economy.

Recent polls from the Pew Research Center and the Council on Foreign Relations show that the percentage of respondents who say the United States should "mind its own business internationally" has spiked higher than at any point in nearly fifty years. Nor is trade as popular as it used to be. Americans are becoming more skeptical that globalization—the increasingly free flow of ideas, information, people, money, goods, and services across borders—is working in their favor.[8] For too many workers in the U.S. manufacturing sector, the cheap products keep coming and the jobs keep going.

Adding to the country's inward focus is the absence of any singular, easily identifiable threat to American security that can rally a broad segment of the public around a more activist foreign policy. China has sharply increased its economic, political, and military clout in recent years, particularly in East Asia, and some U.S. officials will work hard to vilify China and its government—over unfair trade practices, human rights abuses, threats to cybersecurity, and other perceived wrongs. But for the moment, China's stated commitment to a "peaceful rise," its willingness to bankroll so much U.S. debt, and the opportunities China continues to provide for U.S. companies make it difficult to paint the world's most populous country as a Soviet-style supervillain or to conjure up Soviet-scale threats to the international order. China's top leaders do not threaten to bury the United States, they don't bang their shoes on desks at the United Nations, and they aren't looking to base missiles in Cuba.

Islamic militants, ever an elusive enemy, have become a less urgent foreign policy priority, particularly since the 2011 killing of al Qaeda leader Osama bin Laden further undermined public support for an extended troop commitment in Afghanistan.[9] Failed or failing states like Yemen and Somalia can create terrorist safe havens that have the attention of U.S. officials, and countries like Pakistan and Iran pose security challenges of their own. But as the American public loses patience with new troop commitments in Afghanistan and elsewhere, U.S. policymakers will be forced to rely on economic pressure and diplomatic coercion to manage these problems.

In fact, an ever-increasing percentage of Americans are not old enough to remember the Cold War and have not absorbed the idea, as previous generations have, that America plays a unique and indispensable role in promoting democracy and keeping the peace. Another terrorist attack on U.S. soil might reignite public interest in an assertive foreign policy, but it might also do just the opposite, by increasing popular demand for a new brand of isolationism.

If this is bad news for U.S. foreign policy, it is worse news for many other countries, because America has acted for decades as the primary provider of global public goods. The American security presence in Europe and Asia has bolstered confidence in both regions that disputes and tensions need not provoke war. Europe can afford to invest in economic and political union rather than military hardware. The presence of U.S. troops in East Asia reassures the Chinese, Koreans, and Japanese that Japan does not need an army. The U.S. Navy safeguards important trade routes. Washington can't single-handedly halt the proliferation of the world's deadliest weapons; the past two decades have made that clear. But the United States has done more than any other country to ensure that nuclear development in states like North Korea and Iran comes at the highest possible cost and risk to discourage other would-be nuclear weapons states from following their example.

Yet growing public concern over mounting federal debt virtually ensures that the United States will have to become more sensitive in coming years to costs and risks of its own when making potentially expensive strategic choices. At home, presidents will be hard pressed to persuade taxpayers and lawmakers that bolstering the stability of countries like Iraq or Afghanistan is worth the risk of a bloody, costly fight. That means decoupling support for a "strong military," an always popular position, from security guarantees for countries that no longer meet a narrowing definition of vital American interests. As a result, questions will arise abroad about America's commitment to the security of particular regions. Some powerful states will test U.S. resolve and exploit any weakness they think they've found. Few of those who have depended on U.S. strength want a global policeman, but many of them will lack protection against the neighborhood bully. Other countries also have reason to value a strong and resilient U.S. economy. Over the past several decades, U.S. consumers have helped stoke growth in many developing countries, and as Americans scale back their spending, the impact will be felt all over the world.

History has shown that it's never a good idea to bet against the United States. That's still true. America's culture of innovation, its economic resilience, its great universities, and its faith in the future remain impressive. Its commitment to security ensures that even sharp cuts in defense spending can't undermine Washington's global military edge. Its cultural appeal will continue to translate into all the world's languages. This period of transition may ultimately allow the United States to get its financial house in order and reemerge on the international stage with new strength. But Washington has serious work to do to restore confidence in the country's financial foundation, and emerging powers continue to cut into America's political and economic lead.

Don't Look to Europe or Japan

This world without leaders is not simply the story of a downsized America. It will be years before any other country or alliance of countries has the resources and self-confidence to fill the growing leadership vacuum.

Because the G7 is an anachronism, and the G20 is more an aspiration than an organization, some have called for a G3 alliance that enables America, Europe, and Japan to pool their resources to achieve common goals. But the barriers to an effective G3 or anything close to it are formidable. First, as the breakdown in the Copenhagen climate summit negotiations and the onset of the financial crisis made clear, attempts in today's world to meet complex challenges without active cooperation and sacrifice from China, India, and other emerging powers are likely doomed to failure. Second, Americans and Europeans disagree on a growing number of central questions—from the most equitable division of labor within

NATO to how best to revitalize the global economy, regulate banks, and broker peace between Israelis and Palestinians.

Most important, following credit crises in several EU countries, European policymakers face years of bitter bargaining to restore confidence in the Eurozone. The process of recovery may well restore Europe's strength from within, but it will generate considerable mistrust and resentment among European governments along the way. The most obvious friction will come from clashes over policy and political culture between core EU countries, like Germany, which must foot the bill to keep the Eurozone on its feet, and the so-called peripheral countries, like Greece, Portugal, and Spain, which have refused for years to live within their means. Warren Buffett explained the contradiction of the EU monetary union in an August 2011 interview with CNBC: "Seventeen countries that joined the European monetary union gave up the right to print their own money. . . . They linked themselves. They gave each other their credit cards and said let's all go out. And some behaved better than others."[10] There is also the tension within the EU between Eurozone countries like Germany looking to bolster the euro and those like Britain that want no part of it.

Germany is a telling case in point. The nation reemerged from the financial crisis with one of the world's healthiest economies. Thanks to limited exposure to the risky bets of U.S. and other European banks that created a contagion crisis across much of the rest of the continent, Germany has seen growth rebound and wages increase. Its unemployment holds relatively low and its trade surplus remains healthier than that of any other country in the world except China. This success should offer Germany a more prominent global role, but unfortunately for its taxpayers, the Eurozone's weaker economies now rely on Germany's economic muscle to help bankroll the bailouts they need to stay afloat. In that sense, Berlin already has more in common with Beijing than with Washington. Germany's political culture has also become a lot less sympathetic in recent years toward countries that spend more than they take in. Look at recent comments by Germany's finance minister, Wolfgang Schäuble, who stated that it is "an indisputable fact that excessive state spending has led to unsustainable levels of debt and deficits that now threaten our economic welfare."[11]

Not surprisingly, officials in Chancellor Angela Merkel's government have tried to appease German taxpayers and governing partners by promising them a say in how their money is spent. Berlin has refused to simply present bureaucrats in Brussels with cash to use as they think best. Instead, it has insisted that Germany help determine the reform processes within each bailed-out country. So far, so good: Europe's profligate nations will never recover until they tackle spending on government wages, pensions, and health care; the taxes these governments charge their citizens and companies; and other elements of fiscal and banking reform. Yet as long-term austerity measures in the bailed-out countries take a toll on the public mood, local politicians will have added incentive to demonize German attitudes. Bottom line: We can expect to see a lot more near-term conflict inside the European Union and a lot less willingness in Europe to take on outside challenges.

The EU will also be preoccupied with battles over borders. Thanks to the Schengen Agreement—a treaty signed in 1985 (and updated in 1990 and 1997)—citizens of European member states don't need passports as they move from one member country to another. So long as native Europeans were the ones moving passportless across borders, the pact was mostly uncontroversial. But that is changing, in part because protests and violence across North Africa have sent large numbers of people scrambling to escape the turmoil by boat.

In April 2011, more than 20,000 Tunisian refugees managed to reach the Italian island of Lampedusa. Overwhelmed, Italy called on other EU governments to share the burden and accept some of the migrants. No one answered the call. In frustration, Italian officials issued the refugees temporary residence permits and encouraged them to fan out across Europe. France intercepted many of the migrants and sent them back to Italy.[12] A few of the Tunisians began a hunger strike at the Italian-French border. Others made it all the way to Paris, and when French authorities moved to deport them, they occupied an abandoned building and began calling themselves the Lampedusa Tunisian Collective.[13] Far-right European political parties have fanned fears that a flood of refugees will overwhelm already cash-strapped countries. In response, the European Union began considering measures to restore border controls under "exceptional circumstances." Today, a once-expanding European Union is creating new barriers to entry. Far from the exception, such fights are likely to keep Europe turned inward for the next several years.

Nor has there ever been much momentum toward a true common European defense policy that might give the continent greater international influence on security issues. Germany has extremely limited ability to project power abroad, Britain refuses to join, and few European countries can afford to sharply increase defense spending. France, Britain, and other NATO members will act in extraordinary circumstances, as they did in 2011, preventing Libyan leader Muammar Gadhafi from massacring large numbers of his people. But both France and Britain have sharply cut defense spending to restore their federal budgets to health.

Nor is Japan, still the world's third largest economy, prepared to play a more demanding global role. Given its imperial history, Japan, like Germany, has been reluctant to assume a greater international political and military presence. Like the United States, Japan has enormous debt problems that must be addressed. Even if a more ambitious foreign policy enjoyed greater popular support, the country's politics remain deeply dysfunctional. In September 2009, the Democratic Party of Japan won a landslide election victory that ended decades of one-party rule by the Liberal Democratic Party. Yet instead of a two-party system, Japan looked more like a no-party system. The DPJ's first prime minister, Yukio Hatoyama, quickly found himself unable to fulfill campaign promises and became engulfed in a finance scandal. His successor, Naoto Kan, was not much more successful. In August 2011, Yoshihiko Noda became Japan's seventeenth prime minister in the previous twenty-two years—a modern-day Asian record. Add to that depressing mix an economy struggling with weak growth and the public outlay to meet the devastating effects of recent natural and nuclear disasters, and Japan is even less likely to accept greater responsibilities beyond its borders.

For a generation, established powers have treated globalization as a Western game. By welcoming hundreds of millions of new players to the poker table, they hoped mainly to build the size of the pot. That's an attractive prospect for those who make the rules— and those who expect to build the tallest stacks of chips. Operating under a set of guidelines, norms, and institutions created and policed by their home governments, multinational corporations based in advanced industrial democracies eagerly joined the game, lured into the developing world by cheap labor, cheap inputs, a less onerous regulatory environment, and new customers. But the Western way of globalization faces an unprecedented test because the new players want more than a seat at the table; they want to make new rules. They want to run their own games in their own neighborhoods, and increasingly they have the muscle, at least on their home turf, to get some of what they want—particularly when they're prepared to stand together on their demands.

DON'T LOOK TO EMERGING POWERS

If geopolitics were scripted by Hollywood, Brazil might take the lead on global environmental issues, India on worldwide poverty, and China on clean energy. Each has deep experience and a vested interest in the assigned subject, and all of them might help a beleaguered world make large strides forward. But G-Zero is not the feel-good movie of the year, and these and other emerging powers are unlikely to bid for a bigger share of global leadership.

Why? Because they face so many formidable challenges at home in managing the next stages of economic development and in protecting their domestic political popularity. For emerging-market countries, emergence is a full-time job, and the demands it imposes on governments are often at odds with those made by other governments at international summit meetings, like the one in Copenhagen.

China seems particularly well cast in the role of emerging global superpower. Its remarkable three-decade economic expansion, dramatically growing geopolitical clout, and steady increases in defense spending have persuaded some observers to call for a G2, an arrangement in which America and China join forces to unite established and emerging players in an ambitious bid to take on pressing transnational problems.[14] But as Wen Jiabao told the UN General Assembly during a speech in September 2010, "China is still in the primary stage of socialism and remains a developing country. These are our basic national conditions. This is the real China."[15]

For the coming years, China will continue to develop—under the leadership of an authoritarian government that believes the ruling party's monopoly hold on power depends on a rising standard of living and a steady supply of new jobs. Such an agenda creates clear incentives for China to avoid precisely the sorts of sacrifice required for international leadership.

What's more, China's growth looks less impressive on closer inspection. Though it blew past Japan to become the world's second largest economy in 2010, measures of its income per person remind us that political officials in Beijing are right to call China a developing country. In 2010, the IMF estimated China's GDP per capita, adjusted for differences in purchasing power, at $7,519. That's good for a ranking of ninety-fourth in the world, about half the per capita income of Lithuania and one-third that of Portugal.[16]

More to the point, China's leaders have publicly acknowledged that the strategy that generated explosive growth rates for the past three decades cannot lift China to the next stage of its development. To move forward, China must rebalance its productivity away from the booming urban centers of the coast to new cities in the country's central and western provinces, which will require intensive investment in new infrastructure on a scale never before seen. China must change the way the country consumes energy to avoid catastrophic irreversible damage to its air and water and excessive dependence on oil imports from politically unstable places, and it must continue to push its economy up the value chain with unprecedented investment in new-generation information technologies, biosciences and bioengineering, and alternative energy vehicles—tough tasks for a government that remains deeply suspicious of the influence of the Internet.

And China must also create a formal nationwide social safety net for its 1.34 billion people, in a country that has never had one. At the same time, the government must manage expectations among workers for ever higher wages and a steadily improving standard of living, and it must cope with the risks and headaches that come with tens of thousands of public protests each year without fueling organized antigovernment social unrest. China will continue to expand its international presence to develop new commercial ties that can help Beijing accomplish all these goals, but this is not a government with an appetite for heavier global burdens.

True, China's military has become more assertive, even aggressive, in East Asia in recent years. In 2011, the Vietnamese and Philippine governments accused Chinese patrol boats of firing warning shots and even threatening to ram energy exploration vessels operating in or around disputed territory in the South China Sea. No one seems to know for certain who within the Chinese leadership authorized these actions, but it's evident that the country's armed forces want to expand their (already considerable) influence within the governing bureaucracy and to test their regional room for maneuver.

And China is working to build a blue-water navy capable of operating far from its shores. To support this project, the country launched its first aircraft carrier in August 2011. But no one should expect this development to transform China's military capabilities. As aircraft carriers go, this one is hardly state of the art. The *Varyag*, built in the Soviet Union, was first launched in 1988. Ten years later, the Chinese bought the ship at auction for $20 million and announced it would be anchored off Macau and serve as a hotel and casino. Instead, it was adapted to accommodate Chinese fighter jets and first tested in the summer of 2011. By itself, the *Varyag*, now called the *Shi Lang*, won't alter Asia's balance of power. What's more, a blue-water navy has uses that don't threaten anyone's security. The Chinese Communist Party must continue to create millions of jobs each year. To create those jobs, the economy must grow, and to achieve that growth China needs access to oil, gas, metals, minerals, and advanced technology from outside the country. A blue-water navy can help safeguard that access and might one day partner with American vessels to do this.

Beyond this mission, though, why should China take on the risks and burdens that come with heavier responsibilities abroad? The U.S. Navy patrols major trade routes and has helped in the past to limit the risk of conflict in every region of the world. China has benefited from that commitment. Beijing, of course, could dedicate huge amounts of money toward sharing this responsibility, but what incentive does it have to do so? The problem for China, and for everyone else, is that the United States has increasingly limited means to carry this weight—and Americans are likely to retreat from some of their overseas commitments faster than the Chinese, or anyone else, can afford to fill the vacuum.

Bottom line: To conclude from this evidence that the country is building a more expansionist foreign policy is a leap too far. Wars against other powerful countries are dangerous and expensive for a state that needs to keep its economy stable while it undertakes the ambitious economic reforms needed to pull off the next stage of development.

Other emerging players are no more likely than China to take on a global role. Russia's government would very much like to restore some of Moscow's imperial grandeur. To that end, Vladimir Putin has taken a tough line with some of Russia's neighbors. But the country has yet to diversify its economic power much beyond the export of oil and gas, and without the Soviet Union's military clout or its ideological appeal for much of the developing world, Russia can't afford to play the military heavyweight outside its traditional sphere of influence.

Since gaining independence in 1947, India has taken pride in its unwillingness to closely align with any other country. In fact, Jawaharlal Nehru, the country's first prime minister, refused a permanent seat for India on the United Nations Security Council.[17] His successors are far more focused on managing relations with an expanding China and an ever-evolving threat from Pakistan than on expanding the country's geopolitical influence beyond Asia. Significantly, large segments of India's domestic economy remain closed to large-scale foreign investment, limiting the country's leverage in international politics.

Emerging states like Brazil and Turkey are certainly poised to take advantage of new opportunities to play a more prominent diplomatic role, but mainly within their respective regions. For example, Brazil has helped ease tensions between Venezuela and Colombia, while Turkey continues to actively champion the cause of Palestinian statehood. Yet relatively limited means and internal pressures will ensure that both governments pick their spots carefully as they raise their profiles.

No Strength in Numbers

Can the world's leading global institutions fill this leadership void? That's not likely for the foreseeable future. Coordinated efforts to address the questions that matter most for relations among nations and the global economy were once made by the G7—elected leaders and finance ministers of the United States, Japan, Britain, France, Germany, Italy, and Canada, the world's leading industrialized powers. With American leadership, these free-market democracies set the international agenda from the 1970s into the first decade of the new century.

The financial crisis of 2008 put an end to that, accelerating an inevitable transition toward a new order, one that embraced the steadily growing political and economic importance of emerging powers like China, India, Brazil, Turkey, Saudi Arabia, the United Arab Emirates, and South Africa. In November 2008, the G20 came of age as officials from nineteen countries plus the European Union gathered in Washington to pull the global economy back from the brink. Some heralded the G20's arrival as a great achievement, a forum that finally reflected not only the true international balance of power but its social and cultural diversity as well. In 2008, Indian prime minister Manmohan Singh declared, "The G20 has come to stay as the single most important forum to address the financial and economic issues of the world."[18]

Reality has proven more complicated. Only when each member feels threatened by the same problem at the same moment is the G20 apt to make significant progress. Even when financial crisis inspired dread of imminent global economic meltdown, G20 summits in Washington in November 2008 and London in April 2009 produced little more than harmonious rhetoric and modestly positive results. It's no mystery why: Getting twenty negotiators to agree on anything beyond a photo op and high-minded declarations of principle is difficult enough; it's all but impossible when they don't share basic political and economic values. It's like herding cats . . . together with animals that don't like cats.

Leaders of the G7 didn't need to debate the virtues of democracy, human rights, freedom of speech, and free-market capitalism. For all their disagreements on individual issues, America, Europe, and Japan have long since institutionalized these basic principles. The G20 offers a vastly broader diversity of views on these subjects—and the interests of the established and emerging powers around the table are often diametrically opposed. That's one of the reasons why the G20 is fast becoming as much an arena of conflict as a forum for cooperation. Over the next several years, this lack of leadership will have far-reaching implications for all of its toughest challenges.

Then there are the older and more familiar multinational institutions. New Yorkers woke on the morning of May 15, 2011, to news that Dominique Strauss-Kahn, managing director of the International Monetary Fund, had been pulled off a plane and arrested at John F. Kennedy Airport following accusations of sexual assault by a chambermaid at a Manhattan hotel. In the days that followed, the city's tabloids trumpeted each new twist and turn in the case with comic gusto and a seemingly inexhaustible supply of French-themed sexual puns.* But while the media focused on what had happened in that hotel suite, officials in Beijing, New Delhi, Brasília, Moscow, and Pretoria drew attention to an issue of much greater importance: Would the IMF replace Strauss-Kahn with yet another European director? Or might the time have come for emerging powers to break the Western monopoly on leadership of the world's most influential multinational financial institution?

The ease with which the IMF's executive board settled on former French finance minister Christine Lagarde as the new director six weeks later underscores an important fact about today's international politics and its near-term future. While emerging powers have much more influence than they used to, they are hardly on the verge of rendering U.S. and European power obsolete. Despite informal promises from high-ranking European officials when Strauss-Kahn was given the job in 2007 that the next IMF head would be the first from outside Europe, Lagarde became the eleventh consecutive European to hold the post since the fund's founding in 1945.†

---

* The *New York Post* probably pushed the envelope as far as it would go with the headline "Booty Gaul."

† In fact, even before Lagarde replaced Strauss-Kahn, the post had been held for twenty-six of the previous thirty-three years by a French national.

In part, Europeans rallied around Lagarde for local reasons. The IMF's toughest task in July 2011 was to support efforts by European institutions to restore confidence in Europe's peripheral economies by helping to balance the demands of the European Commission, Europe's central bank, and individual governments, particularly Germany and France. But the real reason Lagarde was a shoo-in is that the major emerging-market countries weren't very unified in their opposition and couldn't agree on a serious alternative candidate.

Before the choice of Lagarde was finalized, Chinese, Indian, Russian, Brazilian, and South African officials signed a public letter warning that selection of another European would undermine the fund's legitimacy. With no hint of irony, Chinese officials urged "democratic" fairness in the succession process.[19] Strauss-Kahn's abrupt resignation had caught them off guard, but even if they had had all the time they needed to coordinate a response, they would have struggled to agree on a mutually acceptable nominee. As more emerging powers become international creditors, we can expect a transition toward greater influence for them within these institutions. Yet given the issues that still separate emerging powers from one another, the quick selection of Lagarde reminds us not to exaggerate the speed of that transition or the likelihood that they can work together over the longer term on anything of substance.

Another interesting test of emerging-market strength will come with selection of the next World Bank president, a post held since the bank's founding by an American. Denied the leadership role at the IMF, the BRICS governments (Brazil, Russia, India, China, and South Africa) may feel they have to try to mount a formidable challenge when the World Bank job opens. But this world in transition is not simply an international system divided between established and emerging powers. It's also one in which little unity of purpose exists among governments within these two groups. That can only make it more difficult to shift the balance of power within organizations that were designed seven decades ago to entrench American and European leadership. Failure to rebalance these institutions will encourage emerging powers to withdraw support from them—and to try to build their own.

In the past, developing countries turned to the World Bank and the International Monetary Fund when they needed a financial lifeline. In exchange for loans, these organizations—and by extension the Americans and Europeans who drove most of their decision making—insisted on compliance with specific demands for political and economic reform. That gave the West greater leverage with the rest.

Today, many developing states are looking not to weakened Western institutions but to cash-rich emerging powers to lend them money and to build them new roads, bridges, ports, schools, and clinics without demands for reform or a detailed accounting of how the money is spent. In fact, in its bid to lock in access to all those commodities that the country's economy will need, the Chinese government has become a major international lender. In 2009 and 2010, the state-dominated China Development Bank and Export-Import Bank of China extended more than $110 billion in loans to governments and companies in the developing world.[20] That's more than the World Bank and much more than the IMF doled out over the same period. These Chinese lenders are policy banks; their mandate is to further the Chinese government's political and commercial goals by helping to secure the oil, gas, metals, minerals, and land that China will need to fuel its economy.

Certainly, the World Bank and IMF are not quite as Western-dominated as they used to be. Emerging-market countries like China and India have insisted on and received a much greater say—

in the form of voting rights—within both institutions. China, in fact, now has greater voting leverage within the World Bank than any individual European government and all others except the United States and Japan. Within the IMF, China, Saudi Arabia, Russia, and India all figure among the top eleven members by voting power. This shift is both fair and inevitable. But emerging powers are not satisfied with the scale or speed of these changes, and the diversity of views these organizations now represent further dilutes the efforts of any one country or group of countries to set an agenda within them. That, in turn, undermines their cohesion and effectiveness. As the Copenhagen climate summit illustrated, a diversity of voices is good for maintaining the status quo but bad for management of transnational threats that demand decisive action.

Nor are we likely to see the formation of new alliances outside these institutions that extend much beyond particular issues. Broadly speaking, Europe and America share common political and economic values, but as bickering over NATO operations in Afghanistan and Libya demonstrated, the two sides can't agree on how much each should contribute to coordinated action. Too many member states are reluctant to contribute enough troops, weapons, and matériel to give a security alliance like NATO a coherent post–Cold War purpose.

Among the leading emerging-market powers, the BRICS countries now hold summits and talk publicly of shared interests, but there is much less to their partnership than meets the eye. These countries don't have much in common beyond a shared desire to increase their international influence and to limit the ability of established powers to impose their will on everyone else. China and India are among the largest energy importers. Brazil and Russia are among the world's most important energy exporters, giving them a very different view of policies and events that push crude oil prices higher. China and Russia are authoritarian countries that face internal ethnic and religious challenges to their territorial integrity, while India and Brazil are genuine multiparty democracies with governments that must weigh the need for sometimes painful reforms against frequent fluctuations in public opinion. China and India are rivals for influence in South Asia. China and Russia compete for influence in Central Asia—and in Russia's Far East. Brazil is the only BRICS country that lives in a relatively stable region. China, India, and Brazil each have far more trade with Europe and the United States than with Russia. South Africa, admitted to the group in December 2010, has virtually nothing important in common with any of them.

About the only thing on which major emerging powers *do* agree is that it's time they had a greater say in decisions that will shape the future. But what do they want to say? For the moment, they're not saying.

PROBLEMS WITHOUT BORDERS

Now that the United States can no longer afford the role of global policeman, expect to see plenty of elbows thrown at the regional and local levels as rising players compete for local dominance. With established powers less willing and able to intervene, underequipped local forces will be left to keep the peace, and battles will more often become wars.

Western powers, American or European, have long been reluctant to break up fights outside their regions. Elected officials of the Western powers are well aware that their publics tend to support costly, extended military action only when they believe that vital national interests are at stake. That's why, from the ethnic cleansing of Yugoslavia to genocide in Rwanda and from crimes against humanity inside Sudan to Russia's 2008 war with Georgia, they have remained on the sidelines for as long as they could. But over the next several years we're likely to see both a larger number of local conflicts and an even deeper Western disengagement, particularly in a time of austerity at home.

The United States has withdrawn from Iraq and announced an end date for the war in Afghanistan, leaving overmatched local leaders to fend for themselves against those ready to test their authority. It took the 9/11 terrorist attacks to move America into these countries, and U.S. troops will not return simply to rescue failing governments. In addition, as in Russia's war with Georgia, rising powers will insist on the right to manage their respective regions, and outside actors will offer little more than diplomatic posturing in response.[21] "Never again" will become an even emptier promise because so many cash-strapped established powers and preoccupied emerging states will balk at taking on risks and burdens that others won't be willing and able to share.

But conventional war is not the only—or even the most worrisome—potential source of international conflict. When governments of the leading powers are more worried about creating jobs, building a positive trade balance, and fighting inflation than about the outbreak of war among major countries, the most important instruments of power and influence become economic tools—control of market access, investment rules, and currency policies rather than aircraft carriers, troops, and tanks. As sure as death and taxes, the lack of international leadership will move governments to use oil, gas, metals, minerals, and even commodities like grain as instruments of foreign policy.

In a G-Zero world, great power competition is far more likely to take place in cyberspace than on a battlefield, as state-supported industrial espionage becomes a more widely used weapon in the battle for natural resources and market share. At the same time, emerging players will challenge Western assumptions about banking, telecommunications, and Internet standards, and governments will find new ways to reestablish state control over the flow of ideas, information, people, money, goods, and services across their borders.

We are already witnessing the rise of new barriers and new threats. In both established and emerging states, governments are reasserting their authority. Consider the impact of BlackBerry on both. The governments of India and Saudi Arabia insisted that the Canadian company Research in Motion (RIM) provide them with the tools to intercept and decode BlackBerry messages transmitted within their borders.[22] In response to rioting in London, a British member of Parliament demanded that BlackBerry suspend instant messaging inside the country, and when RIM offered to cooperate with British police, hackers threatened to retaliate. It's not just the free flow of information that has so many states on edge. America complains that the Chinese government is limiting the access of U.S. companies to Chinese consumers, and China counters that America is blocking Chinese investment in U.S. infrastructure and in other economic sectors from energy to telecommunications. European governments face pressure to tighten the EU's internal boundaries. In some cases, public support for this heavier state role could grow as it protects against the turmoil outside.

As individual governments invest less in the global economy and more in their own ability to direct and manage domestic development and the flow of information, the world economy will function a lot less smoothly. We will see politics moving markets much more often and on a larger scale—within both emerging and established powers.

Underneath this era of transition is a moment of painful and costly rebalancing. Some of these high-wire acts have already been mentioned: America must prove that it can continue to meet its long-term financial obligations and restore public confidence in government. China must find a way to shift its economy from dependence on exports toward domestic consumption. Europe needs to ensure that the Germans, Dutch, and Scandinavians don't end up permanently bankrolling a social safety net for the Greeks, Portuguese, and Spanish. These are policy choices, if unpleasant ones born of necessity, but the world is also facing a global rebalancing between countries like America that consume too much and save too little and those like China that consume too little and save too much.

This version of the trend is not the result of policy; it will be an order imposed by economic circumstances over which no one has effective control—and it is only just beginning. Yes, emerging players will continue to see their leverage increase within existing institutions, and they will begin to push for the creation of new ones. But this increase in their rights and privileges will not soon persuade them to accept a more demanding leadership role in international politics.

* * *

We have entered a period of transition from the world we know toward one we can't yet map. Shifts on this scale never come without conflict. But this transition can't last indefinitely, because the inability and unwillingness of established and emerging powers to coordinate and compromise will trigger all kinds of challenges that have to be addressed. A decade from now, some of today's emerging players may begin to look and act a lot more like established powers, and the turmoil that all these problems generate could force a new level of cooperation, maybe even coordination, among the governments of the world's most powerful countries. Or perhaps all this turbulence will reverse their progress, pitting them one against another in a competition for resources and regional influence.

Either way, the damage done between now and then will be determined by answers to a few important questions. In a world without leadership, can America and China build on a mutually profitable partnership, or are the world's leading established and emerging powers on a collision course? Will these two countries emerge from this era with new confidence or new crises? Can Europeans rebuild Europe's core? How many of today's emerging powers will fully emerge? Are we on a path toward global economic and security meltdown?

This is not a story of the decline of the West or the rise of the rest. In years to come, none of these players will have the power to bring about needed change. The G20 doesn't work, the G7 is history, the G3 is a pipe dream, and the G2 will have to wait.

Welcome to the G-Zero.

CHAPTER TWO

The Road to the G-Zero

The reasonable man adapts himself to the world;
the unreasonable one persists in trying to adapt the world to himself.
—George Bernard Shaw, *Man and Superman*

During the 1960s and 1970s, Brazil, Argentina, Mexico, and other Latin American countries borrowed more money than they could hope to repay. The inevitable result: During the 1980s, the region suffered an extended debt crisis. In December 1994, an armed uprising in the southern Mexican state of Chiapas, low world oil prices, hyperinflation, and more than one policy miscalculation pushed the Mexican peso into turmoil. Three years later, in 1997, the collapse of Thailand's currency triggered a financial meltdown across East Asia. The following year, lingering financial effects from the first war in Chechnya, a spiraling fiscal deficit, and a series of erratic political decisions forced devaluation of the Russian ruble and default on Russia's debt.

The circumstances that provoked these crises were quite different. All they really had in common was that they terrified foreign investors and that the United States played an important role in recovery. Some of the help arrived directly from the U.S. Treasury Department, but Washington also rode to the rescue by securing financial backing through the IMF, the World Bank, regional development banks, and other international organizations.

Compare that with America's role in Europe's current debt crisis. Today, the United States is far too busy with its own debt debate to ride to Europe's rescue. Instead, Washington can offer only indirect support, well-intended advice, and political pressure to enact needed internal reforms. That's why in October 2011, French president Nicolas Sarkozy turned hat in hand toward Beijing with a plea for financial help for the Eurozone. He should not have been surprised when Chinese officials agreed only to act as part of a "multilateral" approach, one that would bring in large numbers of other governments and provide China's leaders with domestic political cover should the rescue effort prove a fabulously expensive failure. Beijing knew well that other governments would balk. Their response was simply Chinese for "no thank you."

This is the G-Zero: Everyone is waiting for someone else to put out the fire. How did we reach this breakdown in the international order?

From the Ashes

The road to the G-Zero begins at the height of American dominance. At the end of World War II, much of Europe lay in ruins for the second time in less than thirty years. Even before the war ended, representatives of forty-four nations gathered at the Mount Washington Hotel in Bretton Woods, New Hampshire, to lay the foundation for a new global economy. From the agreement signed there in July 1944 came the International Monetary Fund, the International Bank for Reconstruction and Development (which soon became part of what would be the World Bank), and a plan to establish new commercial and financial relations among nations and set exchange rates that tied the currencies of each member to the U.S. dollar.

The need for reconstruction was everywhere apparent. Vast numbers of the war's weary survivors were jobless, hungry, and desperate. The conflict had cut Europe's agricultural output by half and its industrial production by two-thirds. Even after the fighting ended, food rationing continued and in some cases tightened. Germany was torn in four, with American, British, French, and Soviet zones of occupation. The war leveled a staggering 40 percent of all buildings in Germany's fifty largest cities, the country's industrial production cratered, and around five million of its soldiers were reported dead or missing. Inflation soared, black markets thrived, and cigarettes briefly replaced bills and coins as the street's most valuable currency. In Italy, the war destroyed an estimated one-third of the country's assets, and prices jumped fiftyfold between 1938 and 1948.[1]

World War II cost Japan's emperor more than 80 percent of his empire's prewar Asian territory. Beyond Hiroshima and Nagasaki, many of Japan's largest cities were rendered virtually uninhabitable by U.S. bombing raids. Once known as Asia's workshop, Japan lost 80 percent of its textile machinery. Production of coal, a crucial energy source, fell to one-eighth of prewar levels. As General Douglas MacArthur noted, "Never in history had a nation and its people been more completely crushed."[2]

Yet if men from Mars had landed in Paris, Leningrad, or London in 1945, they would have been hard pressed to tell the victors from the vanquished. The destruction cost France 20 percent of its houses, half its livestock, two-thirds of its railways, and about 40 percent of its total national wealth.[3] Inside the Soviet Union, the war claimed 25 million lives and destroyed 70,000 towns and villages.[4] In the years that followed, the USSR would become a military superpower with considerable international ideological appeal, but the Soviets and their Eastern European satellites would remain burdened for the next forty-five years with a political and economic system that could not create prosperity and could never be sustained.

Nor was Britain spared permanent damage. World War I made the country's superpower status prohibitively expensive, and World War II finished it for good. No longer the world's creditor or its preeminent naval power, Britain faced mounting debt, while its trade was cut to 30 percent of prewar levels.[5] The pound sterling surrendered its international reserve status. Impoverished China, bludgeoned for years by Japanese occupiers, stood on the brink of civil war. India, Indochina, the Middle East, Africa, and Latin America had not yet emerged from the colonial period.

Enter the new superpower—America, the G1. With so much devastation in Europe and Asia and so few countries ready to play an international role, the United States began redesigning the global system to support Washington's goals. The war took a considerable toll on Americans too, but casualty figures were much lower than those inflicted on the countries that provided its frontline battlegrounds, and after a dozen years of depression, the economic surge generated at home to support the war effort lifted American power to unprecedented heights.* The United States cre-

---

* The war cost the United States about one-third of 1 percent of its population. That is a heavy toll, but compare it with the loss of 10 percent of all German citizens and nearly 14 percent of all Soviets.

ated 17 million new jobs during the war to meet skyrocketing demand for weapons and matériel. American salaries doubled, and savings accounts increased sevenfold.[6] The U.S. standard of living rose, and unemployment virtually disappeared.[7]

Armed with these advantages and faced with a choice between retreating into isolationism or expanding its power abroad, the architects of U.S. postwar policy pursued two complementary goals. First, they wanted to build trade ties abroad to avoid a slide back into depression at home, to help create jobs for 11 million returning soldiers, and to extend the economic gains of the war. Second, they sought to promote democracy and thwart communism by containing the risk that European misery might provoke a third and even more destructive world war.

At Bretton Woods, Treasury Secretary Henry Morgenthau Jr. delivered the closing remarks:

> We are at a crossroad, and we must go one way or the other. The Conference at Bretton Woods has erected a signpost—a signpost pointing down a highway broad enough for all men to walk in step and side by side. If they will set out together, there is nothing on earth that need stop them.[8]

The proposed destination was universal peace and prosperity, and the road was mapped and paved by the United States and its European allies.

How the West Was Run

Americans like to believe that their best is the world's best. After all, the U.S. professional baseball championship is known as the

World Series, a name made only slightly less ridiculous by the presence of the Toronto Blue Jays in the American League's Eastern Division.* Then there is the International House of Pancakes, a chain of more than fifteen hundred restaurants whose *global* presence amounts to seventeen restaurants in Canada, twelve in Mexico, and two in Guatemala.[9] Like IHOP and baseball's Fall Classic, the *World* Bank and the *International* Monetary Fund, both headquartered in Washington, D.C., clearly bear the "made in America" label.

Some critics charge that by conditioning financial support to needy countries on adoption of democratic, free-market reforms—an agenda dubbed the "Washington Consensus"—these institutions exist mainly as tools of U.S. foreign policy.[10] That's a caricature, but beyond the succession of Western leaders who have run these organizations, no one can deny that the U.S. and European governments retain formal and informal powers within them that no longer reflect the size of their contribution to the global economy's strength.

These baked-in Western advantages are no accident. At Bretton Woods, most of the other forty-three participating countries gathered around the negotiating table depended on Washington for wartime aid. Call them a coalition of the broke and hungry. As for the American agenda, President Franklin Roosevelt opened the conference with a call for U.S.-led international cooperation. He compared the global economy to the human body:

> *Commerce is the life blood of a free society. We must see to it that the arteries which carry that blood stream are not clogged again, as they have been in the past, by artificial barriers created through senseless economic rivalries. Economic diseases*

---

* Remember the Montreal Expos? They're now the Washington Nationals.

*are highly communicable. It follows, therefore, that the eco-
nomic health of every country is a proper matter of concern to
all its neighbors, near and distant. Only through a dynamic
and a soundly expanding world economy can the living standards of individual nations be advanced to levels which will
permit a full realization of our hopes for the future.*[11]

Roosevelt knew that an increasingly deep-pocketed, self-
confident, and assertive Washington needed free-flowing global
trade and stabilized exchange rates to keep the U.S. economic engine humming, and by 1944, America was calling the shots on postwar planning. Currencies would be pegged to the U.S. dollar,
removing fluctuation and friction from global trade. The dollar
would be convertible to gold at a fixed price. This provided central
banks with monetary wiggle room in a time of crisis, while the dollar's good-as-gold status eased the inflationary concerns that came
with it. This system committed the U.S. government to convert
dollars to gold on request, but because the country held more than
22,000 metric tons of it by the early 1950s—half the gold ever
mined in human history to that point—the day when America
would fail to meet its obligations seemed far beyond the horizon.[12]

The IMF was created to promote the new monetary rules and
lend to countries that couldn't pay their debts. The World Bank
would help finance the reconstruction of Europe before serving as
a provider for other countries in need. Influence within these institutions took the form of voting shares, calculated through a formula engineered by Washington to produce its desired results. The
United States claimed about one-third of IMF and World Bank
votes at their inception. Add the number apportioned to Canada
and America's European allies, and the Western states controlled
nearly three-quarters of the World Bank vote.[13]

Washington was not shy about setting rules within these new organizations to establish lasting U.S. dominance. To veto any proposal within the IMF or the World Bank, a country needed 20 percent of the shares. Only the United States passed that threshold. When the Nixon administration decided in 1969 that the U.S. contribution to the IMF had become too expensive, Washington lowered both the U.S. share and the veto limit.[14] The World Bank followed suit in the 1980s.[15] In both cases, the United States made sure that only Washington held a veto—and the veto ensured that no further changes could be made without U.S. support. Today, despite the increasingly well-documented rise of emerging-market states, Europe and the United States still hold a majority of IMF voting shares.[16]

The United Nations was also built on a foundation of Western values, and as World War II drew to a close, the victors moved to establish their hold on the organization. The fifteen-member Security Council, not the full General Assembly, was granted responsibility for authorizing military action, establishing peacekeeping operations, and imposing sanctions. The United States, Britain, France, the Soviet Union, and China—the only permanent members of the Security Council—were given individual veto power over all UN proposals. Though this structure would soon become a roadblock for U.S. plans, the problem was not immediately obvious. When the council first met in January 1946, China was not yet communist, the Soviet Union was not yet widely recognized as a potent military threat to free-market democracy, and the Cold War had not yet begun.

New institutions were not enough—Washington needed a more aggressive plan to rebuild Europe. In 1947, the value of U.S. imports from Europe was only about half that of its Europe-bound exports. Without a substantial infusion of cash, Europeans would run out of money, and Americans would lose their most likely large-scale trade partners.[17] Adding to the urgency, Soviet troops continued to occupy several Eastern European countries. Communist governments began to appear, and Marxist ideology gained footholds in Western Europe, where economic misery helped build support for communist parties in France and Italy.[18] To halt the advance of Soviet influence and to protect its most lucrative export markets, Washington moved to subsidize European reconstruction on an unprecedented scale.

With a price tag of 10 percent of the U.S. federal budget in its first year, the Marshall Plan allowed the United States to pour an additional $13 billion into Europe between 1948 and 1952.[19] Just as European institutions, the IMF, and Western European powers of 2011 provided Greece with emergency infusions of cash to try to halt the spread of debt crises across Europe's most vulnerable economies, so the United States of the late 1940s provided Greece with military and financial aid to quell riots and halt the advance of Soviet communism.[20]

U.S. investment soon began to pay dividends. By 1952, Western European economies were already operating at double their prewar levels.[21] Washington's willingness to keep troops in Europe provided a security umbrella that allowed Western European governments to focus spending on local economic development. Despite the shadow cast by U.S. and Soviet troops and tanks, West Germany became one of the largest, most dynamic economies in the world, with growth of almost 6 percent a year between 1950 and 1967.[22]

Germany was not the only defeated power to soar from the ashes of World War II. When General MacArthur assumed responsibility for the occupation of Japan in 1945, he outlined America's vision for the country's future in characteristically grandiose terms. He described postwar Japan as "the world's greatest laboratory for an experiment in the liberation of a people from totalitarian military rule and for the liberalization of government from within."[23]

As in Germany, U.S. occupation eased fears among Japan's neighbors of any resurgence of militarism inside the country. It also freed Japan's government of the need to spend huge sums on the country's defense. And as in Germany, within a decade the Japanese people seized the opportunity to build an economic powerhouse. In the late 1940s, U.S. administrators spent $1 million per day to reinvigorate Japan's industrial potential.[24] By 1956, the Japanese government could declare that its people "are no longer living in the days of postwar reconstruction."[25] In the second half of the 1960s, Japan averaged 11 percent growth per year.[26] In 1968, Japan surpassed West Germany to become the world's second largest economy, a ranking it would not relinquish until China overtook it in 2010.[27]

Japan's success with capitalism was not the only source of the country's resurgence. Japan's Ministry of International Trade and Industry (MITI) intervened to manage many aspects of the domestic economy. Much like China's currency policy of the past several years, it supported Japanese exports by pegging the yen to the dollar at an artificially low value. MITI's ranks supplied the country with many of its midcentury prime ministers. Japan's rise also made clear once and for all that nothing barred ancient Eastern cultures from embracing Western capitalist values.

As Japan grew stronger, many Americans began to view its rise as a threat to American hegemony. Yet unlike today's China, Japan's competitive edge flowed from a political and economic system in relative harmony with the Washington Consensus. By the 1970s, Western Europe and Japan were breaking free of postwar U.S.

dominance, but political and economic values helped align their national interests. In 1975, the United States, Japan, Britain, West Germany, France, and Italy formed the G6 group of industrialized nations. A year later, Canada made it a G7. Whatever the economic and cultural rivalries within the group, common faith in free-market democracy and a collective fear of Soviet communism ensured a fundamental unity of purpose.

THE OIL WEAPON

By the time French finance minister Jean-Pierre Fourcade hosted the first G6 gathering at the Château de Rambouillet in November 1975, a crucial ingredient in the Western European and Japanese revival had begun to fuel a direct challenge to Western hegemony. Cheap crude oil was essential for the postwar recovery. In 1948, Japan imported 32,000 barrels of oil per day, just 7 percent of the country's total energy consumption. By 1972, it was importing 4.4 million barrels per day, and oil accounted for about 70 percent of its energy use. The same pattern held in Western Europe. In 1955, oil satisfied just 23 percent of Western Europe's energy needs. By 1972, that had climbed to 60 percent. During this period, global demand for oil, which most often sold for between $2.50 and $3.00 per barrel, grew by 550 percent. Plentiful, cheap crude had entered the industrialized world's bloodstream.[28]

At first, the world's growing thirst for oil further empowered U.S. global leadership. In fact, when World War II began, the United States provided about 63 percent of the world's oil. The Arabian Peninsula, Iran, and Iraq combined to produce less than 5 percent. America and its allies could count on plentiful supplies of cheap crude, and Texas was the world's supplier of last resort. But in 1960, after new discoveries elsewhere in the world had begun to diversify supply, Saudi Arabia, Iran, Iraq, Kuwait, and Venezuela banded together to make better political and economic use of what was fast becoming their lifeblood commodity, and the Organization of the Petroleum Exporting Countries (OPEC) was born. As the world's leading economies deepened their dependence on oil, demand began to grow more quickly than supply.

In its earliest days, OPEC had scant international leverage. Western companies continued to draw the lion's share of profits from new discoveries in the Middle East, and price hikes did little to enrich the developing countries in which oil was produced. The cartel's first attempt at an embargo—during the June 1967 war between Israel and Egypt, Jordan, and Syria—was mostly an embarrassment, but history was slowly moving to OPEC's side. During the 1960s, countries in the Middle East and North Africa ramped up production by 13 million barrels per day, accounting for two-thirds of the decade's global increase in consumption. OPEC member states began to claim a greater share of profits from Western oil companies operating on their territory. By 1972, Qatar, Indonesia, Algeria, Libya, the United Arab Emirates, and Nigeria had joined the cartel.

Then the balance of power between buyers and sellers reached a tipping point. In March 1971, Texas reached maximum productive capacity, unable to increase supply to ease upward pressure on prices. At the time, the United States imported about 3.2 million barrels of oil per day. Over the next five years, that figure nearly doubled, and OPEC gained crucial market leverage. With each passing year, the cartel's output decisions became more critical to the stability of oil and gasoline prices in Europe and the United States. The turning point came with the Yom Kippur War in October 1973, another Arab-Israeli conflict that provoked OPEC to again test its oil weapon. This time, the cartel members discovered they had the power to inflict real pain on the world's most powerful economy. In retaliation for Washington's support for Israel, OPEC members cut oil shipments to the United States and incrementally removed oil from the market at large. Weeks before the war and embargo began, oil sold for $2.90 per barrel. By the end of the year, the price had quadrupled.

Just as oil markets reached a game-changing moment earlier than most expected, so too did the central contradiction of the Bretton Woods Monetary Agreement. The system it created depended for stability on a U.S. commitment to provide two reserve assets, dollars and gold. Both were offered at a fixed price—gold, for example, could be redeemed at $35 an ounce—but while the supply of dollars was flexible enough to meet changes in demand, the supply of gold was not. In the late 1960s, U.S. government spending, particularly on the Vietnam War, fueled deep current-account and trade deficits. Inflation surged, and several European governments, concerned by a depreciating dollar and unwilling to weaken their own currencies to preserve the peg, demanded gold in exchange for large amounts of their dollar reserves.

In response, President Richard Nixon terminated the Bretton Woods agreement. On August 15, 1971, he moved to "suspend temporarily the convertibility of the American dollar into gold or other reserve assets, except in amounts and conditions determined to be . . . in the best interests of the United States."[29] Though the White House described the move as temporary, it has never been reversed. Two subsequent devaluations of the dollar—making U.S. exports more competitive and undercutting the value of foreign countries' dollar reserves—marked the death of an accord that had produced decades of prosperity. Inside the United States, these multiple moves were largely swallowed up by the din of the war and its protesters. Outside, the move became known as the "Nixon Shock."

Why, asked OPEC officials, should we exchange our most precious resource for a currency that's rapidly losing its value? The oil embargo, and the price spike that came with it, sent some of the world's leading economies into a tailspin. Between 1973 and 1975, U.S. GDP fell by 6 percent while unemployment doubled. Japan's economy recorded its first losing year since World War II. OPEC members meanwhile saw their fortunes rise. Sharply higher prices more than offset the drop in export volumes, allowing cartel members to sell less and still make more money. Their oil revenue climbed from $23 billion in 1972 to $140 billion in 1977. The Americans and Europeans had nuclear weapons, but OPEC's leading members had discovered they had a kill switch that could quickly send Western economies into recession.[30]

Having made its point, OPEC lifted the embargo in March 1974. The damage to other currencies done by the Bretton Woods peg to a declining U.S. dollar, President Nixon's decision to "close the gold window," the havoc wreaked by the oil embargo, and the willingness of America's European allies to withdraw support for U.S. policy in the Middle East to protect their own oil supplies underlined an emerging reality: Few will follow a leader who isn't leading toward the promise of peace and prosperity. Cold War pressures had provided many governments with ample incentive to rely on and support American strength, but once that strength appeared to waver, as it did during the 1970s, support became conditional.

As the West's thirst for oil lifted one set of challengers, its hunger for consumer products empowered another. In East Asia, as Japan became more prosperous and its workers earned higher salaries, manufacturing became more expensive, and the costs were passed on to foreign consumers. That created an opening for the so-called Asian Tigers: South Korea, Taiwan, Hong Kong, and Singapore. The lower cost of production in these countries made for cheaper products that found eager buyers in America and Europe. At Bretton Woods, the United States had pushed for open markets to build consumer demand for U.S. exports. Three decades later, manufacturing hubs in the developing world and wealthier U.S. shoppers had reversed the flow of trade. In 1960, Americans spent $15 billion on imported products. By 1985, that number had reached nearly $340 billion.[31] That's how the Asian Tigers became the world's first emerging markets—and Washington lost a little more of its political leverage.[32]

How did the tigers earn their stripes? Combined with Japan, they represent less than 4 percent of the world's population and less than 1 percent of its land.[33] With so few available resources, these countries had little choice but to look beyond their borders for growth opportunities. Between 1970 and 1987, the four Asian Tigers more than doubled their share of world exports.[34] At the same time, they used subsidies and trade barriers to protect local companies from foreign competition until they had grown ready to compete.[35] The transformation of trade balances was most apparent with the United States. In the process, the tigers racked up an enormous balance-of-payments surplus.* Thailand, Malaysia, the Philippines, and Indonesia followed the path blazed by the original four. As the United States fell more deeply into debt, the list of emerging markets grew longer and these smaller countries took a larger share of global wealth. With so much activity in the neighborhood, the sleeping giant next door began to awaken.

---

* From 1970 to 1986, the U.S. share of the tigers' exports increased from 22 percent to 37 percent, while the American share of their imports declined from 32 percent to 17 percent.

EVERY NATION FOR ITSELF

ENTER THE DRAGON

China's rise began in 1976 with the death of Mao Zedong. A year later, China still accounted for just 0.6 percent of world trade.[36] In 2010, it surpassed Japan to become the world's second largest economy, and Western bankers and economists are now taking bets on just how soon China will claim the title of the world's largest trading nation.[37]

Beginning in the late 1970s, Mao's successor as paramount leader, Deng Xiaoping, began the reform process by establishing four "special economic zones," coastal enclaves that served as capitalist laboratories where foreign companies were invited to invest on favorable terms. Spurred by early success, Deng gradually expanded the experiment. In 1984, fourteen coastal cities were opened to a surge of foreign investment. In the countryside, agricultural production soared as new rules gave farmers new freedoms and new incentives to produce. As with Japan and the Asian Tigers, trade expanded and manufacturing boomed.

Economic change created social problems. The injection of huge amounts of money into China's labyrinthine bureaucracy created corruption on a massive scale. In a country with little history of labor mobility, mass migration brought tens of millions of peasants from rural backwaters into the boomtowns of the southern and eastern coasts. A spike in social unrest followed as the gap between rich and poor widened and already populous cities became dangerously overcrowded. Political leaders who feared that the party would lose control of all these changes grew even more anxious as a different form of experimentation sparked turmoil inside the Soviet Union. Divisions emerged within China's leadership over how much and how fast the country could afford to change.

On April 15, 1989, Hu Yaobang, a senior party official who had been purged and publicly humiliated for his support of political liberalization, died following a heart attack. A spontaneous gathering of students and intellectuals began in Beijing's Tiananmen Square on the eve of his funeral. Demonstrations took on a life of their own over the next seven weeks, as swelling crowds in Beijing and other major cities around the country demanded various forms of political and economic change. On May 20, the Chinese leadership declared martial law in an unsuccessful bid to force protesters to disperse. Two weeks later, on June 4, the army broke through human blockades and entered the square, killing an unknown number of people, injuring many more, and setting back the process of reform for several years.

Later that year, China's leaders watched as Hungary's embattled communist government opened the country's border with West Germany. Huge numbers of East Germans crossed into Hungary and then to the West, rendering the Berlin Wall obsolete in a matter of hours. Peaceful uprisings swept the Warsaw Pact governments into history. Two years later, the Soviet Union imploded. China's conservatives feared for the future, but the country's reformers looked to learn from the failures of European communism to deliver on promises of a better life for ordinary citizens. Deng's reforms were delayed, but their early success and Deng's persistence ensured they would not die. The events in Tiananmen Square ultimately persuaded China's leaders that an isolated economy would eventually breed rebellion, and the opening up to trade outside China's borders that followed gave the Asian giant unprecedented economic power.

VICTORY AND FRAGMENTATION

After more than four decades of confrontation and bloody proxy wars across the developing world, the collapse of European and Soviet communism and the end of the Cold War appeared to usher in an era of American dominance. U.S. politicians championed a new form of manifest destiny, one in which an exceptional, ascendant superpower would inspire followers on every continent to remake the world in America's image. Russia, heart of the Soviet empire, was invited to expand the G7 to a G8 to ensure that Moscow did not lurch back toward communism or turn to military rule. The Wall fell, and fears of nuclear winter gave way to a promising spring.

But Cold War victory restored neither international harmony nor American preeminence. Instead, it simply speeded the rise of a new generation of increasingly self-confident emerging-market countries, each with its own values and vulnerabilities. From the ashes of the Soviet Union itself came fifteen new states. Some (the Baltic states, Ukraine, and Georgia) turned toward Europe. Others (Belarus and Armenia) clung closer to Russia. Most, including energy-rich states like Kazakhstan, Turkmenistan, and Azerbaijan, opened to foreign investment from several directions. In Russia itself, the economic upheaval of the Yeltsin years gave way to the era of Vladimir Putin and a revival of centralized state power. The rise in oil prices during his presidency filled Russian coffers with cash, giving the country a new political stability and self-confidence.

Germany's reunification laid the foundation for a nation that is again the powerhouse of Europe and accelerated progress toward European expansion. In 1992, the Maastricht Treaty created the European Union, the world's largest consumer market, and led to the creation of the euro, a common currency that, despite the recent financial problems of some of its seventeen member countries, has already become an alternative to the dollar as an international reserve currency. With more than 500 million citizens in twenty-seven countries, the EU is home to the world's largest middle class and has become the world's most peaceful and prosperous region.

China, Brazil, and India are now among the world's ten largest economies, and Russia, Mexico, South Korea, Turkey, Indonesia, and Poland are among the next ten. Little wonder that most of these newly empowered countries are increasingly assertive in staking out a foreign policy agenda that is driven neither by alliance with superpower benefactors nor by ambitions to join the established powers' clubs. Jawaharlal Nehru established the independence of India's foreign policy in the late 1940s. Now that his country is one of the world's most important emerging economies, its guarded approach to partnerships with other powerful states has become a much more significant factor in regional and international politics.

Brazil's surging economy and its growing global profile have elevated the nation to Latin America's most influential power and generated pride across the country. In 2010, then-president Luiz Inácio Lula da Silva demonstrated his nation's independence and growing clout—and a willingness to infuriate U.S. and European negotiators—by joining with Turkish prime minister Recep Erdoğan to broker a deal with Iranian negotiators in the multinational standoff over Iran's nuclear program. This is not a deal that Turkey would have sponsored when its ambition to join the European Union trumped its drive to become a regional power broker, but as in Brazil, growing economic and political self-confidence has encouraged a popular elected government to raise the country's prestige.

In short, globalization—a phenomenon championed by Washington for both political and economic reasons—has created multiple emerging alternatives to American power, including a loose collection of developing countries with leaders looking to satisfy public demand for a more prominent global role by dabbling in international politics. They want status. They feel that their growing economies should win them greater respect on the international stage. Yet these new players balk at assuming the risks and burdens that come with a share of global leadership, focusing instead on managing each delicate stage of their countries' economic development. This reluctance is at the heart of the G-Zero.

NUCLEAR DIFFUSION

Few challenges illustrate the dangers of a world without leadership more vividly than the proliferation of the world's most dangerous weapons. In 2009, a previously unknown computer worm known as Stuxnet suddenly infected tens of thousands of computers in more than 150 countries. Though some experts called it the most sophisticated malicious computer program ever seen, this weapon did not draw much media attention until experts discovered that among its many features is an ability to send nuclear centrifuges spinning out of control.[38] As a result, many analysts now believe it was designed as part of a joint U.S.-Israeli project to disrupt the nuclear program under development in Iran, and senior U.S. and Israeli officials have since reported their belief that Iran's uranium enrichment program has been significantly delayed.

All this amounts to high, if mostly hidden, drama, but it's just the latest episode in the nearly seven-decade battle to contain one of the world's most complicated long-term problems. The two bombs that abruptly ended World War II marked the peak of

American military dominance, but the U.S. atomic monopoly lasted just four years. The Soviets successfully tested an atomic device in August 1949, and the race was on to bolster national defenses with the most destructive available weapons. Britain joined the club in 1952. France followed in 1960, and China crossed the threshold in 1964. These five countries then looked to award themselves the same advantage they continue to enjoy within the United Nations Security Council—a veto. In 1968, a number of countries, including the United States, the Soviet Union, and Britain, signed the Nuclear Non-Proliferation Treaty (NPT), which recognized their status as nuclear weapons states. France and China added their signatures in 1992. In total, 189 states have now signed the treaty, which provides members with the internationally recognized right to "peacefully use nuclear technology" for energy and research in exchange for a pledge not to develop or traffic in nuclear weaponry.[39]

The trouble with the NPT is that no one has the power to guarantee enforcement of its terms. Like Israel, India, and Pakistan, any nation's leaders can refuse to sign the treaty and dare the world to punish them for it. Israel is widely believed to have developed a nuclear capability during the 1960s, though its government has never formally confirmed that.[40] During one tense week in May 1998, rivals India and Pakistan rattled the world with dueling underground nuclear tests. Or, like North Korea, a country can join the NPT and then renounce it when the weapons are ready. North Korea's government, which ratified the agreement in 1985 and abruptly withdrew in 2003, is believed to have proven its nuclear weapons capability with a test in October 2006. Or, like Iran, a government can simply join the club and cheat. Iran signed the NPT in 1968 but is generally assumed to be hiding an aggressive push to develop a nuclear weapons program.

In a G-Zero world, the enforcement of existing rules will demand a unified approach to coercive diplomacy. Only a united front will be forceful enough to persuade a government like Iran's to renounce its permanent guarantee against conventional military attack and accept a public rebuke in front of its people. Yet creating a new, more credible nonproliferation regime would demand a degree of compromise among established and emerging powers that is no more likely than a credible climate change agreement.

In turn, the spread of nuclear weapons will exacerbate another problem. Two kinds of power determine international politics: the power to force change and the power to resist it. In the G-Zero, no government or alliance of governments has the power to enforce nuclear nonproliferation, while a growing number now have the means to resist. When it comes to hard power—the military and political means to coerce another government to do something it wouldn't otherwise—a nuclear weapons capability is the ultimate defense. North Korea has one, Saddam Hussein did not, and Iran can see the difference. That's why, short of a regime change and perhaps not even then, the Iranian government is extremely unlikely ever to negotiate away its nuclear program.

At the same time and for some of the same reasons, emerging countries have an interest in engaging Iran's government. They need the oil and gas that Iran can produce in abundance, they want access to what could become a fast-growing consumer market, and they want influence with a government that remains a major regional player. Developing states also share an interest in limiting the ability of established powers to gang up on a fellow developing state. That's why, in the G-Zero, sanctions on would-be weapons states will be harder than ever to enforce—and at a time when the pace of technological change accelerates the process of proliferation.

Rogues like North Korea and Iran have earned their reputations as international outlaws, but they do have at least one valid

NPT-related complaint. The five recognized nuclear states agreed by signing the treaty to work toward eventual disarmament. Though the Strategic Arms Reduction Treaty of 2010 placed new limits on their respective stockpiles, the United States and Russia still have nearly 20,000 nuclear weapons between them, more than 95 percent of the world's total.[41] That, too, is not likely to change anytime soon.

U.S.-China Frictions

Rhetorical flourishes (from both camps) aside, Beijing has had good reason to value American power and Washington's willingness to use it over the past thirty years. A generation ago, China's state-owned enterprises and political bureaucrats had little experience with potentially volatile emerging states in Africa, the Middle East, Southeast Asia, and Latin America, not to mention moving tankers through troubled waters. America's willingness to play the global policeman has given China time to open and maintain trade routes and sea lanes, and develop trade and investment relations abroad. The willingness of successive U.S. presidents to pull punches on Beijing's human rights record in favor of better trade relations created the makings of, if not a beautiful friendship, at least a profitable partnership.

Despite the delay imposed by events in Tiananmen Square, the death of European and Soviet communism helped the aging Deng Xiaoping persuade China's elite that only a rising standard of living would save the country's one-party system and that a more ambitious experimentation with market-driven capitalism was the only way to get there. To create jobs, Beijing worked to open consumer markets around the world, especially in America and Europe, to

Chinese exports. The drive to build a modern economy also required a warm welcome for foreign companies that could provide Chinese companies with access to state-of-the-art technology, management and marketing expertise, best commercial practices, and unprecedented levels of foreign direct investment.

Following Deng's death, Jiang Zemin and his allies within the leadership extended and expanded these plans. U.S. manufacturers won access to cheap Chinese labor. American consumers got imported products at low prices, which helped keep inflation in check even as America's economy was booming. China's surge filled the country's factories with millions of new workers each year,[42] and its government purchased enormous quantities of U.S. debt, financing still more American consumption of Chinese-made products—a virtuous circle, at least for China.[43]

In 1999, the need to fuel further development persuaded the leadership to adopt its "Go Out" strategy. State-owned energy and other enterprises were dispatched around the world in an unprecedented push to secure long-term supplies of oil, gas, metals, and minerals. Two years later, in 2001, China joined the World Trade Organization, agreeing to abide by established commercial standards and to accept the institution's authority to enforce its rulings. The achievement was hailed on both sides of the Pacific. By allowing China to protect its hard-won gains and to build a capitalist future on a solid foundation, American power proved indispensable for China's expansion, and many American companies gained access to China's fast-growing middle class. The two countries' economic interests were increasingly aligned, and China did not yet have the political or economic muscle to create strategic competition between them.

Things change. The upheaval that comes with three decades of double-digit growth has transformed China. The anxieties generated by profound economic and social changes, a growing wealth gap between the coast and the countryside, severe damage to China's air and water, disputes over land rights, endemic corruption, and dozens of other issues have provoked considerable unrest in recent years, and these problems have remade America's relationship with China.

To ensure a more "harmonious" rise and to reduce the uncertainty caused by so much economic change, a new generation of Chinese leaders has pushed over the past decade for a more direct state role in managing China's expansion. No one knows better than China's current leaders that command economics can't produce lasting long-term growth. But they also know that if markets are allowed to determine winners and losers on their own, the state could lose control of the resources needed to stimulate its economy and create jobs during a crisis. Were that to happen, market forces could then empower those who might use their newfound wealth to challenge the Chinese Communist Party's monopoly hold on domestic political power.

That's why the party has moved in recent years to tighten its grip on the processes of economic development. The use of national oil companies allows the leadership to ensure that China's long-term energy needs are met, in part by arming these firms with the financial resources and political influence they need to secure contracts with the governments of commodity-producing countries. Other state-owned enterprises and politically loyal national champions bolster the state's ability to direct resources and create jobs to reinforce stability. State-run banks and sovereign wealth funds help ensure that capital is directed to support these and other projects. A growing number of Chinese companies have become much more competitive and now see foreign companies not as potentially useful partners but as rivals for local market share, and they're using political connections within the bureaucracy to craft investment rules and regulations that favor local firms at the expense of their foreign competitors. Currency policy is directed toward ensuring that growth remains steady and predictable. In short, China has embraced state capitalism, a system in which the state dominates local market activity for political gain, and China is becoming an increasingly complicated place for many American companies to do business.[44]

The 2008–2009 financial crisis added to the friction by underlining China's dangerous dependence for growth on suddenly cash-strapped U.S. and European consumers. Just as critically, the financial market meltdown also marked a turning point in the U.S.-Chinese balance of power, stirring anxiety in Washington and a more patronizing approach from Beijing. Upheaval in the Arab world in 2011 heightened the Chinese government's risk aversion and further limited its (already low) tolerance for any hint of organized political dissent. Meanwhile, the growing self-confidence of China's diplomats, its business leaders, and its people has also changed Beijing's attitude toward Washington and U.S. companies. A swelling national pride, expressed most vividly in the triumphalist pageantry of the 2008 Beijing Olympic Games, segued into criticism of U.S. policy, following the onset of the financial crisis and during the 2011 fight in Washington over the U.S. debt ceiling. In response to the debt ceiling issue, Xinhua spoke of a United States that was "kidnapping" the global economy: "The ugliest part of the saga is that the well-being of many other countries is also in the impact zone when the donkey and the elephant fight . . . the potential collateral damage is way too heavy."[45] China's assertiveness provoked resentment in the United States, adding further fuel to the fire.

More troubling, the growing divergence of U.S. and Chinese

economic strategies created by the clash between U.S.-style free-market capitalism and China's state-dominated version is fast becoming a source of serious instability. During the Cold War, Western and Soviet bloc economies operated mostly on separate planets; outside of Soviet oil and gas exports, there was very little capitalist-communist trade. But the U.S. and Chinese economies are now moving in different directions only after establishing a deep economic interdependence. It will be years before Washington has restored enough fiscal discipline to rebuild confidence in the country's long-term economic dynamism. China may need even longer to significantly ease its dependence on access to Western consumers for growth. Chinese exporters have enough allies within the political bureaucracy to water down reforms, and because the process could force dangerous numbers of Chinese factory workers out of their jobs, the leadership is likely to move slowly and carefully. In the meantime, the conflicts between U.S.- and Chinese-style capitalism and the ability of politicians in both countries to exploit public resentment of the other will make matters worse.

American Free Fall

The financial crisis accelerated an already inevitable shift in the world's balance of political and economic power from a U.S.-dominated global order toward one in which emerging powers have become indispensable for real solutions to a gathering storm of transnational threats. It's a transition from a global economy driven by the increasingly free flow of ideas, information, people, money, goods, and services toward a system in which governments are using old tools in new ways to maintain political control in the face of rapid change. In Washington, policymakers who once debated how best to wield America's unmatchable power must cope with self-doubt and second-guessing. Politicians still talk of American exceptionalism, but mainly to ward off fears that it no longer exists. Declarations of superpower dominance have given way to whispers of default.

Americans aren't worried simply by the rise of potential competitors. They're also concerned that the American dream is no longer within reach. The cumulative impact of the loss of so many manufacturing jobs over so many years, the depth and duration of the economic slowdown that followed the financial crisis, the frustratingly tepid pace of recovery, and fears for the country's ability to pay its long-term debt have taken a serious psychological toll. Worse still is the fear that America's leaders can't fix these problems because the U.S. political system is broken beyond repair. Washington's partisan paralysis of the past several years doesn't inspire much confidence that help is on the way.

Decision making in Washington has added to America's troubles. When he became president in January 2001, George W. Bush inherited an economy in recession. The tech bubble had burst, and the U.S. economy was sputtering. The financial impact of the September 11 terrorist attacks made matters worse. It's hard to argue that Bush and the Republican-led Congress were responsible for either of these disasters, though their policy responses to them did substantial long-term damage to America's fiscal health. The Bush administration launched two wars and an unfunded benefit plan for prescription drugs even as it enacted one of the largest tax cuts in American history, inhibiting the government's ability to pay for either conflict. Spiraling deficits became a defining feature of U.S. foreign policy. Barack Obama, who inherited both wars and an economy in free fall, spent much of his time and attention during his first year in office on the passage of health care reform rather than on much-needed changes to international financial market rules or on policies to kick-start long-term economic growth.

But the problem didn't begin with George W. Bush or Barack Obama. In 1980, the United States was the world's largest creditor nation. By 1987, it was the world's largest debtor nation, with a trade imbalance that soared to $170 billion. Republicans will blame the Democratic Congress of that period. Democrats will counter that President Ronald Reagan never once presented the Congress with a balanced budget. Neither side is wrong. Successive presidents and Congresses of both parties have allowed government spending, especially on entitlements, to spiral out of control.

America can recover its strength. Its economy will be the world's largest for years to come, and access to American consumers will remain a powerful attraction for the economies of many established and emerging states. In a leaderless world, Washington will continue to act as "leader of last resort," particularly when military might is what's needed and a credible case can be made that vital U.S. interests are at stake. Washington can afford to spend much less on defense without sacrificing its capacity to project power across land, air, and water in every region of the world.

In short, the end of American dominance does not mean that Uncle Sam is now just one of the guys. No one knows yet which emerging states can prove their long-term staying power. Existing international institutions can't take up the slack because they have adapted hardly at all to the sweeping changes of the past several decades. The diffusion of international power since the end of the Cold War, which sharply picked up speed with the onset of the financial crisis of 2008 and the volatile global economic conditions since then, has created a vacuum that no one is yet fully prepared to fill.

This brings us to the growing number of immediate challenges that no country can take on alone. Reliance on a leader of last resort won't be nearly enough. The G-Zero is more than a state of mind. It's about to create crises and opportunities on an enormous scale, and from surprising directions. The next chapter details both.

CHAPTER THREE

The G-Zero Impact

What begins in fear usually ends in folly.
—Samuel Taylor Coleridge, *Table Talk*

In 2011, a package with nearly undetectable plastic explosives hidden in printer cartridges was checked on board a UPS cargo plane from Yemen through London bound for Chicago. The plot was foiled only when a Saudi intelligence tip helped British authorities intercept the package. Even after security officials at East Midlands Airport found the right cargo container, they struggled to identify the individual package within it that held the bomb. Officials later learned that they had inadvertently deactivated the bomb just three hours before it was set to explode by separating the cartridges from the printer during the search.

We won't always be so lucky. In 2010, the world's thirty busiest airports alone handled more than 50 million metric tons of cargo, and the security chain is only as strong as its weakest link.[1] Maintaining the highest level of safety is expensive, and governments that don't feel directly threatened by terrorism have few good reasons to accept the cost. Even if the United States could afford to underwrite security in every port and airport in the world, with plans and procedures that conform to an American standard, the U.S. willingness to pay would encourage every other government to spend that much less on security—and counterterrorism efforts would still depend on the willingness of local officials to share information, to use new technologies correctly, and to enforce all the rules all the time. Complicating matters further, past U.S. attempts to gain information on passengers boarding U.S.-bound flights in Europe have run afoul of European privacy laws.[2]

Persuading states around the world to share the costs and burdens that come with a uniform screening standard for people and packages that travel by air or sea has never been more important, but when it's every nation for itself, this will be more difficult than ever to accomplish.

In this and countless other ways, the G-Zero stands to change our lives. To prevent wars among powerful nations, to keep the peace in cyberspace, to enable global trade, to protect the environment, and to ensure that people across the developing world have enough food and water at prices they can afford, the world needs leadership. We're not going to get it. Instead, the G-Zero will create multiple, often interlocking international challenges, complicate many that already exist, and make all of them more difficult to meet.

Established powers no longer have the political and economic muscle to impose and enforce rules or to drive a global agenda. Equally crippling, the development needs of emerging powers will lead their governments to reject calls for the sorts of collective international action that demand sacrifice. We'll focus in this chapter on the G-Zero impact in the three most crucial areas: the most likely arenas of state-to-state conflict, the fight over global standards, and the implications for the most basic of all necessities—air, food, and water.

BATTLEGROUNDS—REAL AND CYBER

The Middle East and Asia on the Brink

In a G-Zero world, the Middle East and Asia will generate more turmoil than any other regions. The upheaval that brought down governments in Tunisia, Egypt, and Libya in 2011 will continue to ripple through the Middle East—and at a moment when the United States is reducing the size of its footprint there. U.S. forces have left Iraq, and U.S. policymakers are now less willing to devote time, energy, and resources to help maintain stability in the region. Nor will European, Chinese, and Russian leaders fill this emerging vacuum.

Local powers Saudi Arabia, Turkey, and Iran are left with greater influence, but they have often competing goals for the Middle East. Heightened tensions between Saudi Arabia and Iran will play out in places like Iraq, Syria, and Bahrain, and Iran will suffer much more factional infighting as its next presidential election looms large. Egypt's path to democracy is unlikely to prove peaceful, Syria's civil war will intensify, and Israel will feel increasingly isolated. Even relatively stable countries like Morocco and Jordan could face near-term challenges.

The Middle East is the more imminent risk, but nowhere is the longer-term threat of armed conflict greater than in Asia. Asia is home to more hot spots, rising powers, and potential conflicts than any other region and is crucial for the strength of the global economy. Increasingly dysfunctional North Korea might eventually stumble into war. It might also simply collapse, creating a refugee crisis and an enormously expensive reunification project with South Korea. Pakistan has an unpopular civilian government, a feeble economy, a military that regularly interferes in politics, activist judges with political scores to settle, tribal militants, the world's worst domestic terrorism problem, deteriorating relations with Washington, and a stockpile of nuclear weapons. Rivalry and grievance might one day generate another Indian-Pakistani confrontation. Chinese conflicts with Japan, Vietnam, and the Philippines over maritime boundaries and control of natural resources have eroded relations between China and these countries.

Simply put, Asia has too many powerful states and not enough cooperation. China would like to become the dominant regional power, but India is too big to simply accept a secondary role. Japan remains one of the world's wealthiest and most influential countries. South Korea is a leading emerging power. Indonesia is becoming a major economic and diplomatic player.

Hot spots and jostling powers aside, the central problem in Asia is that many countries want to maintain security ties with the United States even as they expand trade relations with China. That isn't sustainable, because Beijing's economic influence gives Chinese policymakers ever-increasing leverage with these governments. As China's consumer markets take on added weight and Americans see their purchasing power reduced, East Asian countries are rushing to expand trade ties with one another and with China. In fact, according to Xinhua, in 2010 China became the largest trading partner and the single biggest export market for Southeast Asian countries.[3] China's agreement with members of the Association of Southeast Asian Nations, which went into effect in 2010, involves more people than any other trade deal in history.

Washington is losing leverage on more than just trade. Given new limits on America's means and the scale of its domestic challenges, officials in Japan, South Korea, Singapore, Indonesia, Thailand, and other U.S.-friendly states can be excused for questioning America's long-term staying power. In fact, China's navy has become more aggressive in defending its territorial claims in recent years in part to gauge the degree of pushback from Washington and its Asian neighbors. Japan doesn't have an army, because the U.S. presence assures that it doesn't need one, but over time, concerns about the U.S. commitment to Asian security could sharpen the Chinese-Japanese rivalry—and even set off an arms race. The Obama administration has worked hard to increase U.S. leverage in Asia—with everything from an agreement to station U.S. troops in Australia to progress on a Trans-Pacific Partnership, an agreement designed to grow regional trade and investment ties among Asian and Pacific Rim countries. But a reduced defense budget will only increase the uncertainty about Washington's commitment to Asia's security.

This brings us to Asia's biggest G-Zero question. One effect of a world without global leadership is that regional powers and organizations could fill the vacuum left by increasingly outdated and dysfunctional international institutions and bring some order to each region. Brazil might fill that role in Latin America. The European Commission and European Central Bank can join with international institutions to bolster the EU and the Eurozone. Saudi Arabia is using the Gulf Cooperation Council (GCC)—an expanding club of Arab monarchies that includes the United Arab Emirates, Kuwait, Bahrain, Oman, and Qatar—to help maintain political and economic stability in the Gulf (though not yet, to be sure, more broadly across the Middle East). Even in Africa, a continent long considered hopelessly fragmented and politically chaotic, Nigeria, South Africa, Kenya, Ethiopia, and Uganda are playing larger constructive roles in managing conflict in their respective subregions. But Asia has too many powerful countries and too few referees: there is no Asian Union on the horizon or even an Asia-wide security forum to resolve inevitable conflicts.

The G-Zero produces paralysis at the global level, creating opportunities for coordination in most regions, but the Middle East is too divided and Asia is too big for that. As American influence wanes, the potential for conflict will grow. The Middle East crises will continue to dominate headlines and roil markets, but Asian conflict will be the biggest global hazard in the years to come.

Cyberthreats

The most underrated arena for conflict in a G-Zero world, especially one in which the United States will remain the world's only global military superpower, is cyberspace. Over the past decade, the threats that increasingly skilled individual hackers and organized criminals pose for businesses have grown, but the risks have been commercial and social, not political. Two factors are changing that. First is the convergence of systems onto the Internet—of power and utility systems (with the move by so many countries to the use of smart grids to manage electricity generation), and information systems more broadly for major sectors of the economy (with the shift to cloud or network-based computing). These trends provide attackers looking to strike at governments or large populations with plenty of tempting and accessible targets. Second, governments themselves are moving aggressively into cyberspace. International politics and cybersecurity have begun to collide.

Threats to stand-alone computer networks have existed for years, but a sophisticated 2007 attack on Estonia's parliament, banks, ministries, newspapers, and broadcasters, suspected to have come from inside Russia, and the previously mentioned Stuxnet worm attack on Iran's nuclear program have underscored the reality that offensive cybercapabilities are outpacing the construction of defenses. As infrastructure networks like power grids are digitized—i.e., made "smart"—and the number of entry points expands exponentially, entire systems will become more susceptible to cyberattack.

Don't misunderstand the stakes: The vulnerability and the potential value are enormous. The worldwide market value of smart grids is expected to rise from nearly $70 billion in 2009 to $170 billion by 2014. The United States and the European Union are leading the way in the deployment of smart grid technologies to link users to power plants, even as guidelines for regulating them are still being written. The U.S. National Institute of Standards and Technology has identified 137 data-exchange interfaces, each of which poses a potential entry point for a cyberintruder. The decentralized structure of the U.S. power sector would probably limit the scope of possible attacks, but a growing number of industry experts believe this threat is underappreciated, especially given the speed at which offensive capabilities are evolving. At his Senate confirmation hearing in June 2011, Defense Secretary Leon Panetta said that the "next Pearl Harbor we confront could very well be a cyberattack that cripples our power systems, our grid, our security systems, our financial systems, our governmental systems." Europe's larger networks and the ongoing political push for a pan-European electric system push the risk of attack there even higher.

Hackers aren't the only threats here. Governments are also developing offensive (often unidentifiable) computer capabilities as a new way to project power in a world where direct military strikes are much more expensive and exponentially more dangerous. During the Cold War, the risk of mutually assured destruction made nuclear weapons all but unusable. Everyone knew when and from where a missile was fired and could retaliate in kind. That's not true for cyberweapons. States are now in the process of putting national cybersecurity strategies into place. The creation of a separate U.S. cybercommand in 2010 reveals a growing military emphasis on cyberwarfare. Other governments, particularly in Europe and Asia, are following suit.[4]

In a world dominated by the West, the United States and its allies might work together to shield public resources, like power grids, from cyberattacks, but in a G-Zero world they aren't likely to succeed in a consistent and coordinated way. As with terrorism, attackers have to hit the target only once to do enormous damage. Past efforts to develop treaties or common codes of conduct have produced little real progress, mainly because states don't perceive their vulnerabilities in the same way or with the same urgency. These vulnerabilities have also fueled the growth of a cyberwar industry, one in which fear of the unknown feeds demand for all kinds of offensive and defensive weaponry—tools created by companies that may not be particular about whom they're willing to include on their expanding list of customers.

In addition, the high-stakes commercial conflict between state-owned companies and multinational corporations is providing state capitalists with a serious home-field advantage. Multinational companies already face a growing need to protect themselves against cyberattacks that are launched, or at least supported, by governments. High-tech businesses are especially vulnerable because the information they hold is unusually valuable for political officials who want to promote domestic industries or bolster national security.

Multinational firms will work together and with their governments to strengthen their defenses, but Western companies doing business inside the world's most technologically sophisticated authoritarian regimes will always be vulnerable. Google and many other major multinational companies have suffered increasingly sophisticated cyberattacks aimed at stealing key technologies.* Recent attacks are among the most effective ever seen in the corporate world, but that's a record made to be broken.

Finally comes the threat posed by info-anarchists and technically sophisticated criminals. In 2010, WikiLeaks founder Julian Assange barely missed becoming *Time* magazine's Person of the Year after the release of thousands of politically sensitive documents badly embarrassed Washington and other governments around the world.[5] In 2011, efforts by several governments to shut him and WikiLeaks down made him the world's first cybermartyr. In response, an army of info-anarchists operating under the name Anonymous launched cyberattacks on those governments and denial-of-service attacks on financial services companies PayPal and MasterCard after they severed ties with WikiLeaks.

Other companies have become targets of online criminals. Sony has suffered raids on personal information involving tens of millions of customers. JPMorgan Chase and Best Buy have reportedly faced similar attacks. Hackers targeted communications of about three hundred major corporations in a single attack on the Nasdaq, one of the world's largest stock exchanges. U.S. congresswoman Mary Bono Mack reported during a meeting of the House of Representatives' Subcommittee on Commerce, Manufacturing and Trade that in a single month in early 2011, thirty cyberattacks on U.S. government offices, banks, insurance companies, hospitals, airlines, and universities compromised about 100 million records. Press reports claim that U.S. government offices suffer about 60 million cyberattacks *each day*.[6]

---

* Google is among the few willing to discuss this issue publicly.

It's worrying enough that in all these forms of (usually anonymous) cyberattack—whether state versus state, company versus company, or individual versus anyone—offense is way ahead of defense. It's even more troubling that no one really knows whether any of these attacks could have been defeated with existing technology and greater vigilance. Without effective deterrence, offense-dominated environments tend to breed fear and overreaction—and the G-Zero dilemma is that every government and institution will defend itself at the expense of others rather than cooperate to design an effective system of collective defense against a common threat.

TRADE AND COMMERCE

The prospect of battleground conflicts—on earth and in cyberspace—may spike the blood pressure, but the most consequential arena of G-Zero competition and confrontation is the global marketplace. Since the end of the Cold War, unrivaled U.S. military power has pushed the governments of some emerging states to look for low-cost ways to boost their international clout and to level the competitive playing field. Even today, no country can afford to spend more than a small fraction of what America invests in its military. In fact, despite the worst U.S. economic slowdown in decades and the rise of emerging powers, the United States still spends more on its military each year than the world's next seventeen biggest spenders combined.[7]

Nuclear weapons offer a potent form of defense, and China and India both have them, but the hundreds of millions of consumers joining fast-expanding middle classes in these countries are what really powers the increase in their international importance. Growing market power in Brazil, Indonesia, Turkey, and other emerging economies has boosted the influence of these countries as well. Bottom line: In a G-Zero world, it is economic muscle, not military might, that determines the international balance of power. For foreign investors, Russia's most attractive assets are its enormous reserves of oil and gas. China's are the potential size of its consumer base and its inexpensive labor force. Knowing this, these and other governments now treat foreign access to their companies, consumers, and natural resources as the most valuable weapons at their disposal.

The result will be a surge in global protectionism. During volatile economic times, political leaders are more likely to safeguard local jobs and their own popularity, and the G-Zero makes this trend much more difficult to combat. To rebalance their books, governments of most of the world's established powers will spend less money. As historically high unemployment rates continue in the United States, Americans will be more sensitive than ever to the loss of jobs to the developing world and to foreign investment from countries that are perceived, correctly or not, to be competing unfairly (think China) or to pose risks for U.S. security (China, Russia, and Arab countries).[8] That has already added pressure on U.S. lawmakers to adopt a go-slow approach on new trade deals. We'll also see more protectionism in Europe, where governments continue to impose tariffs designed to protect local steelmakers, textile manufacturers, and farmers against competition from lower-cost producers.[9]

This protectionist trend will extend to the emerging powers as well. Every government worries that an economic crisis will put too many people out of work all at once and exact a heavy price on the popularity of the country's leaders, but emerging powers usually have greater incentives to protect their markets. Their fortunes can change much more quickly than in established powers; their gains are more vulnerable to sudden reversals. This is especially true for countries like China, Russia, Venezuela, and Saudi Arabia that practice state capitalism, because state companies and banks are more responsive to the political interests of policymakers than to the warning signals provided by markets. But it's also true for a liberalized democracy like France or Brazil, where government is less shy than in the United States about direct state involvement in coordinating corporate strategy to serve the national interest. For all these reasons, we won't see a new global trade framework. Instead, we'll have a series of commercial agreements between individual countries and among small groups of countries that create new investment limits and new trade barriers for those outside the bloc.

There are other reasons why the rise of the rest will fuel the growth of more protectionism. U.S. and European multinationals often use their political and financial influence within Western governments to lobby against protectionist rules and regulations, not because they want to promote the power of the global economy to lift all boats, but because their profits depend on their ability to move products across borders, to import materials and equipment, and to operate supply chains in several countries at once. Globalization drives their growth.

In many developing countries, state-owned companies and privately owned national champions have a very different set of interests. In early stages of development, openness to foreign companies and investment can help boost economic growth and provide local companies with access to good ideas and new technology. But as these economies and companies begin to come into their own, competition from outsiders becomes an obstacle to further growth. Local firms discover that they can expand their market share in fast-growing domestic markets and can use their influence with local policymakers to keep the foreign competition at a disadvantage.

State-owned companies have a further leg up when competing

with multinationals in other countries because they have the financial, political, and diplomatic backing of their governments to a degree that Western companies can't match. Protectionism often works in their favor, and it's especially easy to practice and enforce in countries where courts rarely rule against the state or in favor of a foreign company or investor at the expense of a domestic one. The threat alone that government will change the rules of the game to favor local companies discourages some foreign competitors from challenging them.

How can governments boost domestic producers at the expense of foreign competition? They can slap quotas on certain imports or impose tariffs that make them relatively more expensive than similar products made by local companies. Governments can also use subsidies or loan guarantees to boost local exporters or impose artificially high health and safety standards on certain types of foreign-made products, or they can order local banks to favor local borrowers, move money through state-owned banks to hide subsidies for exporters, or simply refuse to enforce existing rules that protect foreigners and their intellectual property.

These governments also know that the value of their currencies is an important factor in how well they compete, and they will intervene in foreign-exchange markets to protect local exporters at the expense of outsiders. Some in Washington have complained loudly and often in recent years that China holds the value of its currency artificially low to boost its exports, flooding U.S. markets with cheap Chinese products, undermining U.S. manufacturing, killing American jobs, and driving America's trade deficit to new heights. Senior officials in emerging powers like Brazil and India have added their voices to the growing chorus of complaints.[10] American politicians of both parties have threatened punitive action against China, and other governments may begin to retaliate against Beijing by intervening more directly in their own currency markets to offset China's expanding economic power.

As Chinese workers demand higher wages and a better standard of living, many multinational companies are already turning for lower-cost labor to Indonesia, Thailand, and Vietnam. These countries will try to use new rules and regulations to lock in their advantages at China's expense. Even some Chinese companies are now shipping jobs to Thailand, Vietnam, and Myanmar. In a G-Zero world, without a framework in which to manage all this competition, such issues are likely to become a source of serious tension in Asia.

China's success may provoke conflict outside Asia as well. Though Beijing doesn't condition loans to other governments on the sorts of political and economic reforms often demanded by the IMF, the money does come with strings attached. When China invests billions in new roads, bridges, hospitals, ports, and airports in Africa and Latin America, it often insists that Chinese material and workers are used to build them. As locals in these countries discover that Chinese workers are depriving them of land and jobs, they pressure their governments for protections. When they don't get them, some turn to violence. In years to come, we can expect a spike in both political pressure on China from the governments of other developing states and angry demonstrations targeted at Chinese workers living in other countries.

STANDARDS

Why do we care about international standards? Because when the rules of the game are simple, uniform, and universally accepted, trade in ideas, information, goods, and services costs less and produces less conflict. But in a G-Zero world, who decides how to make ports and airports secure? Who sets international technical standards, and why do they matter? Who decides how a cell phone works, how the World Wide Web will develop, and how all those communications-enabled consumer products flying from factories in one country to families in another are made safe?

Ironically, the international standard that emerging-market governments complain about most is the one most likely to survive the G-Zero. The U.S. dollar continues to provide stability for the global economy. Despite the dismantling of the Bretton Woods agreement, U.S. dollars made up more than 60 percent of all the currency reserves held by foreign governments and central banks in 2011, providing a stable store of value during a turbulent moment for the entire economic system. A big portion of global trade is still conducted entirely in U.S. currency, simplifying transactions and reducing costs of exchange. About 85 percent of the world's foreign-exchange transactions involve the trade of other currencies for dollars.[11] That's why foreign governments need a steady supply of greenbacks, and why they're still willing to trade tangible assets for U.S. currency that the Treasury Department can print at low cost.

The dollar's global role has given Americans some important advantages. Steady foreign demand for U.S. Treasury bonds helps keep U.S. interest rates low and enables Americans and their government to borrow money cheaply and to spend beyond their immediate means. Foreign demand for dollars stabilizes the currency's value, helping Americans afford imported goods and keeping prices lower for products made at home. The dollar's privileged status also allows U.S. consumers, companies, and banks to avoid the costs and risks that come with any exchange of currency. Many commodities, including crude oil, are priced in dollars. Thus, even though energy costs for U.S. consumers are determined mainly by the same shifts in supply and demand that affect all consumers, Americans don't have to worry that currency volatility will make matters even more unpredictable.

The dollar has also served over the decades as a global public good, allowing the United States to play the role of lender of last resort, providing foreign investors with liquidity and confidence in times of crisis. That advantage was never more obvious than during the global financial market meltdown, an event triggered by the collapse of U.S. financial institutions, when huge numbers of foreign investors bought dollars as a hedge against the risk of financial upheaval throughout the world. Dollar dominance has been good for Americans, and it has offered security for foreign governments and investors as well.

Nothing lasts forever. A number of emerging powers have begun to insist in recent years that the dollar's singular status provides Washington with a privilege it no longer deserves and that America's mounting debt ensures that the dollar is no longer a stable enough store of value to serve as the world's dominant reserve currency. "They [the United States] are living like parasites off the global economy and their monopoly of the dollar," said Vladimir Putin in 2011. "There should be other reserve currencies." In 2011, as federal debt climbed toward 75 percent of U.S. gross domestic product, critics at home and abroad questioned the willingness of Washington's feuding lawmakers to pay the country's bills and the long-term impact of the country's political stalemate on the value of the dollar.

But the greenback has maintained its decades-long incumbency in part because there has never been a viable single alternative to it. During the Cold War, the shadow of Soviet tanks undermined long-term confidence in West Germany's deutschmark, and Japan avoided pushing the yen as a reserve currency to keep tighter control of its value. The euro has become an alternative reserve currency in limited quantities, but recent debt crises in Eurozone countries have undermined confidence that the single European currency is here to stay. China has taken concrete steps in recent years to advance the yuan as an international currency, but next steps would force a degree of foreign involvement in Chinese markets and a transparency in Chinese policymaking that will be hard for risk-averse Chinese officials to accept anytime soon. That helps explain why, even when the United States is helping to create international market turmoil, investors continue to treat the dollar as the safest port in any storm.

COMMUNICATIONS

High-Tech Trouble

For the moment, the international standards under greatest pressure are those involving global competition in the communications and information sectors—and the largely ungoverned virgin expanse of the Internet. The view from the boardrooms of Western multinationals is that internationally recognized standards, built from bottom-up consensus, make cutting-edge innovation possible. When companies and governments accept a common set of technical standards, they accelerate the pace at which interoperable tech products come online and create and maintain a network of equipment industries that supply lower-cost parts and products that meet those standards. If every country imposed its own guidelines, products would become much more expensive for companies to produce and consumers to buy, creating drag on the entire global economy. So say those who drive the world's advanced industrialized economies, the same mostly Western powers that have been setting global standards since the end of World War II.

Enter now a host of new voices: Beijing, Brasília, Moscow, and other emerging-market capitals agree that global standards are important. But why do Americans and Europeans get to set them? Chinese officials, in particular, argue that U.S. and European companies protect their commercial privileges by forcing Chinese companies to take on the added cost of ensuring that products meet Western specifications. Their U.S. and European competitors then charge billions of dollars in licensing fees for use of their intellectual property. Beyond the financial stakes, some Chinese officials believe that the West wants to "contain" China's rise, by limiting (or even reversing) its economic gains and by using technical standards as a weapon of cultural imperialism.[12]

Political officials in China, for now the only emerging power with enough market muscle to effectively challenge Western standards, are pushing ahead with plans to promote "indigenous innovation," a set of policies designed to help China's economy climb the value chain.[13] New rules mandate that the Chinese government will buy certain types of high-tech products only if they contain a fixed percentage of Chinese-made technology. Less formal policies encourage foreign companies to compete with one another for access to Chinese markets by offering to develop advanced technology inside China, sometimes in coordination with Chinese partners. Foreign firms know that the security of their intellectual property is constantly at risk inside China, but many continue to pay this price as the cost of access to hundreds of millions of Chinese consumers and relatively inexpensive Chinese labor.

The logic behind China's indigenous innovation strategy is simple: Why pay someone to use their technology when you can build lasting economic power by developing your own? Chinese companies have proven again and again that they can adapt and steal technology created by others, but if China can build its own high-tech sector and create domestic standards that give local companies big competitive advantages, the country can take the next step toward becoming a twenty-first-century economic powerhouse. China can then use its new clout to export this commercial advantage by pushing other countries to adopt its standards, allowing Chinese companies to force Western competitors in Asia, Africa, Latin America, and everywhere else to take on the added expense of adjusting to compete in a game made in Beijing. That's a test that many Western multinationals have never faced, and in a G-Zero world no government, alliance, or institution will have the strength to do much about it.

Unfortunately for global growth, China's opaque, top-down approach to standards-setting is not designed to manage the complexity of real-time innovation and the sheer speed of technological change. Government bureaucracies, especially those charged with ensuring that technical advances conform to both commercial and political goals, can't keep pace. This gathering speed and growing complexity multiplies the number of unintended consequences that one badly designed regulation can produce. Then there's the sheer number of Chinese officials with a say in how standardization policy is created and the diversity of their motives. More often than in America or Europe, the policies this generates in China are the product of awkward political compromise rather than economic efficiency.[14] Foreign companies don't want to have to conform to the requirements of such a clumsy bureaucratic process, and they worry that China's state-driven model will provide Chinese companies with influence over the standards-setting process and early access to information that gives them a head start as they move to market.[15]

Beijing has accepted Western safety standards for many low-tech consumer products, mainly because China's economy will depend heavily for the foreseeable future on exports of these goods to customers in Europe, America, and Japan. But Beijing's much more aggressive approach toward pushing its own standard for a variety of higher-tech products has only just begun. A bid to replace the Wi-Fi wireless standard with China's version, known as WAPI, failed. China's government, which owns all three of the country's telecom giants—China Telecom, China Unicom, and China Mobile—was more persistent but ultimately unsuccessful in trying to win international adoption of its third-generation (3G) mobile phone standard, known as TD-SCDMA, in part because technical issues forced years of delay prior to launch. The battle along the next frontier—4G products—is now under way.

The Internet

The Internet wars already emerging in a leaderless world are especially worrisome. In 2009, a public outcry forced Beijing to abandon plans to require that all new personal computers in China, including those imported from outside the country, be equipped with content-control software with the comically Orwellian name "Green Dam Youth Escort."[16] State officials claimed the filter was needed to block pornography, but that failed to quell an intense public outcry and suspicions that Green Dam might be used for other forms of censorship—or even for surveillance. This time, the state backed down. But the fight continues, and governments around the world are trying to restrict the online flow of ideas and information, and in a G-Zero world the battle for control of the Internet could literally dismantle the World Wide Web.

In 1937, the writer H. G. Wells in his essay collection *World Brain* offered this prediction about the future of information:

The whole human memory can be, and probably in a short time will be, made accessible to every individual. This new all-human cerebrum need not be concentrated in any one single place. It need not be vulnerable as a human head or a human heart is vulnerable. It can be reproduced exactly and fully, in Peru, China, Iceland, Central Africa, or wherever else seems to afford an insurance against danger and interruption.[17]

As in other areas, Wells proved prescient. Though the Internet's development was a direct result of years of U.S. government funding and research, this network of interconnected networks was designed specifically to grow without a central operator—the better to ensure organic growth of both commerce and free speech. For more than fifteen years, the Internet's backbone and its technical resources have been commercially operated in a private-sector-led universe in which industry, government, and civil society each have influence.

To date, creation of technical standards has been managed by the Internet Engineering Task Force (IETF), a diverse group of network designers, operators, vendors, and researchers operating under the aegis of the Internet Society, a nonprofit organization that strives "to make the Internet work better by producing high quality, relevant technical documents that influence the way people design, use, and manage the Internet." In the early 1980s, the need for an authority to assign unique name and number identifiers for IP addresses gave rise to the Domain Name System, and in 1998 the U.S. Department of Commerce contracted with the Internet Corporation for Assigned Names and Numbers (ICANN) to oversee this process. The U.S. government has strongly supported the multi-stakeholder approach to the Internet, encouraging it to grow with minimal involvement of political officials, foreign or domestic.

But even as the Internet has become central to communication and commerce in almost every country on earth, unprecedented threats have arisen in cyberspace that compromise personal privacy, the intellectual property of companies, and the security of nations. Criminals, anarchists, and terrorists have used the Internet for profit, power, and ideologically motivated destruction. At the same time, governments have discovered both opportunities to use the Internet for their own purposes and vulnerabilities that must be protected. Those that can afford it have begun to develop the technology needed to militarize cyberspace. Today, ICANN faces considerable pressure from several governments, particularly China and Russia, to provide tools that enhance their "information security," a move that amounts to a declaration of sovereignty over sections of the Internet and the beginnings of a surveillance society online.

The threats that governments are trying to manage via the Internet include some that almost anyone would consider legitimate, like terrorism, and others more likely to excite controversy, like control of political activism. But the Chinese, Russian, and other emerging-market governments want tighter control of the Internet itself. They now argue that the UN's International Telecommunications Union (ITU), a venerable institution originally created during the early days of the telegraph, should become the forum in which governments manage not only the technical aspects of the Internet but also policy issues associated with its growth and the security challenges it creates.[18] This transfer of responsibility would represent a fundamental change in governance of the Internet, because the ITU includes only governments among its members. Representatives of the private sector and nongovernmental organizations have no vote within it and no other means of protecting the interests of individuals and companies.

The need to develop new, secure Internet protocols to combat threats to cybersecurity is as important for America and Europe as for China and Russia, and states will have a larger role to play in developing them. But how much is too much? The world's leading authoritarian governments have a vested interest in using the bureaucratic process of a UN institution to build walls (or back doors) in cyberspace, or top-down-designed technology architectures that slow (or even halt) the free flow of ideas, information, goods, and services across borders.

Some of those walls are already under construction. Best estimates suggest that every twenty-four hours, about 100,000 Chinese log on to the Internet for the very first time, joining the 450 million Chinese already online. The sheer size of this daily wave makes it impossible for Chinese security officials to monitor everything that is said, read, and exchanged online. This gives ordinary Chinese a freedom of speech they didn't have ten years ago. More worrisome for state officials is that cyberspace offers real estate for a virtual public square where Chinese can gather to exchanges ideas and opinions. Freedom of speech is threatening; the more immediate worry is freedom of assembly.

To manage this problem—and any risk it might pose for the ruling party's hold on power—the state relies on a variety of technical tools, including control of Border Gateway Protocols (BGPs), the software that routes online information. Internet service providers and traffic routers use BGPs like maps to move data from one computer to another as quickly and easily as possible. To freeze the flow of data among routers within their control, those who control these systems need only hide the map. For example, when unrest gathered momentum in Egypt before the ouster of Hosni Mubarak in February 2011, his government used this method to shut down the Internet across the entire country. But where Egypt swings an ax, China has learned to wield a scalpel. BGPs provide Beijing with the filters needed for its Great Firewall, the system designed to prevent users inside China from gaining access to content that their government doesn't want them to see.

By manipulating Border Gateway Protocols, China can hasten a shift from a single global Internet to what some now call the "Splinternet," a fragmentation of what was once a unified online universe.[19] In a G-Zero world, the Splinternet will reflect the ability of governments to claim control of discrete segments of cyberspace so that they alone can decide what citizens living within their territory can and cannot access. Iran's government, already one of the world's most sophisticated Internet censors, wants to take this idea to its logical extreme by creating a "national internet," an enclave in cyberspace that would leave Iranian users cut off from the rest of the online world. This project, said Iran's head of economic affairs in May 2011, will create "a genuinely halal network, aimed at Muslims on an ethical and moral level."[20]

Information

In the West, this splintering of content access has begun in more familiar ways. One brand of mobile device comes with default access to a particular search engine or a particular operating system because one company signed a deal with another that provides for exclusive licensing rights. But if companies have commercial motives for creating bordered communities that include some services and exclude others, authoritarian governments have political motives for doing much the same thing—to maximize state control of information.

Paranoia can be a powerful motivating factor. In 2002, the Kremlin informed the Peace Corps, a U.S. government–created volunteer service organization, that it was no longer welcome in Russia. Various explanations for the ejection were offered, but some officials openly accused the organization of spying for the U.S. government.[21] Some in Russia and China now warn that Twitter and Facebook are subtle and insidious instruments of the same American aim. Even those less susceptible to conspiracy theories know that these companies provide citizens inside authoritarian states with news, ideas, and opportunities for communication that might undermine state political control—and Western multinationals, and perhaps the U.S. government, with a treasure trove of information on life inside these countries.

As governments build new walls in cyberspace or require multinational companies to locate equipment within their borders, cross-border flows of information will come under increasing threat. No state has the power to return its people to a world without cyberspace. For almost all the world's governments, blacking out the Internet is a viable option only under the most extreme of circumstances and for a limited amount of time, since blocking the flow of data halts the flow of commerce, depriving the state of the revenue it needs to survive. (North Korea is the exception because it has virtually no commercial flow.) Savvy Internet users around the world have also proven remarkably resourceful at evading state censorship, and state bureaucracies aren't well equipped over the long run to keep pace with technological change. But governments have already proven willing and able to manipulate public access to some information while denying it to others. This trend will create dangerous tensions within many authoritarian countries as the game of cat and mouse breeds suspicion and frustration on both sides.

It won't be easy. The world's most capable authoritarian regimes once held near total control of the information that crossed borders and the ability of private citizens to communicate with one another and with the outside world. Twenty years ago, a coup attempt in the last days of the Soviet Union triggered a good old-fashioned race to the state-run television station and an armed confrontation over control of the airwaves. There was no satellite television with news and views from abroad, no mobile phones, no text messages, no Internet, no YouTube to share secretly recorded images, and no Twitter to produce constant updates on everything from everywhere. The few Soviets able to pick up Voice of America radio had a single alternative source of news.

Those days are long gone. The Chinese, Russian, Saudi, and Iranian governments can monitor, filter, and reroute, but they can't return to the day when most messages with political content were broadcast from a single state-controlled radio or TV tower. With the exception of North Korea and a few other isolated outposts, communications have become profoundly decentralized.

The information revolution is an entirely different story. The traffic data and content produced by all the world's emails, online searches and purchases, and the electronic signatures from all those texts and tweets can now be aggregated in real time and stored in a central location. Those with access to that data—and the technology to organize and use it—have captured something extraordinarily valuable. To date, most of it is held by large (mainly Western) corporations. These firms are subject to various privacy and security rules, but they can still use the information to make money. As we're reminded with every new pop-up ad, mining our data reveals our interests and preferences and helps those who process it target advertising toward us. Google's dominance of the search space makes it the world's largest source of advertising revenue. Facebook has become a store of information on individual consumer preferences and trends on a scale unmatched in human history—it is disconcerting to think of advertisers as Facebook's customers and its user base of more than 800 million people as its product.[22] Thus, while some within authoritarian regimes consider these companies to be Western troublemakers, others in those same governments see them as banks of priceless political and security information.

As we use new communications tools to reveal more of who we are, what we think, and what we want, data analysis will become a source of much greater interest—and not just for multinational companies looking to build market share. Providing those who think of us primarily as consumers with so much data might compromise privacy, but passing that information to governments—to those who think of us as citizens, voters, organizers, opinion makers, *or* potential troublemakers—is another matter entirely. True, governments around the world can meet the needs of their people more effectively if they know more about them. Collection and interpretation of personal data can help policymakers design systems to help street traffic flow more freely, target infrastructure investment, fight crime, and safeguard national security. But how does the state draw a line between activists and criminals? Or terrorists? Or potential terrorists? Each government will use this material in its own way. Both established and emerging world governments are prone to abuses of power and violations of the rights of the individual, and as states get more deeply involved in data collection, security officials will want maximum control of everything they consider relevant for (what they consider) national security.

Google has already endured multiple attacks on the Gmail accounts of suspected dissidents inside China, attacks engineered (or at least condoned) by Chinese authorities. Imagine the pressures that any foreign communications company will face if Chinese citizens use it to discuss politics and organize protests (of any kind). These tensions are already a central fact of life for many authoritarian governments learning to cope with the faster flow of data across borders.

A Hostile Environment

Climate Control

No G-Zero problem is more painfully obvious than the inability of established and emerging powers to agree on a credible plan to tackle global warming. Data from the International Energy Agency showed a record surge in carbon emissions in 2010, but efforts to halt climate change have made virtually no progress since the failed summit at Copenhagen in December 2009. In Durban, South Africa, in December 2011, negotiators agreed to extend the Kyoto Protocol through 2017—without the support of key players like Canada, Japan, and Russia. They join the United States on the sidelines as America famously refused to even ratify the original 2005 agreement.

Many emerging powers still want to extend the Kyoto Protocol because it requires developed states to make the largest sacrifices in the name of limiting emissions. After all, say China, India, and others, the West is responsible for most of the environmental damage of past decades. They're the ones who should do the most to clean it up. Americans and Europeans counter that this division of responsibilities no longer makes sense. It's time for a new treaty, they argue, because the emerging powers will be responsible for most of the greenhouse gas emissions in decades to come. While Kyoto has been thrown a lifeline beyond its 2012 expiration, its survival is largely meaningless in driving global emissions reduction.

Durban avoided the tough choices, leaving climate change policy with no guiding framework for the foreseeable future. When states' interests are so divergent and no one can force them into line, the tough choices won't stay on the table long.

Beyond Kyoto, the United States and China hold the key to breaking the deadlock in international negotiations, given that they alone account for 40 percent of global greenhouse gas emissions. But Washington and Beijing are locked in a policy catch-22: If China refuses to take on major new obligations, the U.S. Congress will never ratify an agreement or move forward on domestic carbon pricing; and if the United States does not undertake credible emissions reduction measures, China can hide behind U.S. inaction and avoid new responsibilities.

One of the few positive developments to come from Copenhagen was a promise by established powers to provide developing countries with $100 billion a year by 2020 to help pay for the changes needed to reduce emissions. That figure included $30 billion in "fast track" financing for 2010–2012. At another climate summit in Cancún, Mexico, in 2010, negotiators debated the establishment of a Green Climate Fund to provide more financial help. This is a classic example of a global public good, the kind of service that benefits everyone and for which no one wants to pay. But here again the G-Zero rears its head. Established powers have yet to agree on how to divide the cost among governments and between the public and private sectors. As is the case with so many aspects of the G-Zero, sharp cuts in government spending in both the United States and Europe—and the unwillingness of some in Washington even to acknowledge that global warming exists—will only make matters worse.

As some states accept that global warming won't be resolved at the international level, we'll see efforts within individual countries to adapt to these changes. Some governments will mandate that various products that use energy must meet efficiency standards unique to that country. Energy efficiency is important, but from air conditioners to refrigerators to automobiles, when multiple countries impose multiple standards, the cost of doing business can become prohibitively expensive.

More worrisome still is the likelihood that some governments, fearful of the long-term environmental damage that climate change will inflict and confident that no global solution to the problem is possible, will invest in "geoengineering," the science of climate manipulation. Scientists are already debating both the viability and the ethics of efforts within individual countries to manage climate emergencies by spraying sulfate aerosols into the upper atmosphere to reflect solar radiation back into space.[23] How might this practice in one country impact its neighbors? What are the long-term effects of this practice? Do we understand the adaptability of the earth's atmosphere well enough to allow individual governments to take actions that might have global and permanent effects? In a G-Zero world, with countries left to manage global challenges on their own, we might not know until the damage is done.

Climate change is also creating opportunities—for example, by making the Arctic a much more accessible place. Since 1980, the average annual reach of Arctic sea ice has retreated by about 8 percent—an area larger than Norway, Sweden, and Denmark combined.[24] Yes, these rising sea levels portend a world of trouble, but receding ice also grants potential access to new, perhaps vast deposits of oil, natural gas, and other valuable commodities on the sea floor and opens new international shipping routes that will be passable for longer periods of the year. For the United States, Russia, Canada, Denmark, Norway, Iceland, Finland, and Sweden—members of the Arctic Council, a forum for countries with claims to Arctic territory—competition for land, water, and resources is heating up right along with the temperatures, and the stakes could be extraordinarily high.

There will be a lot to fight over. Estimates vary, but according to the U.S. Geological Survey, the Arctic could hold as much as 30 percent of the planet's undiscovered natural gas reserves and 13 percent of its undiscovered oil. For the moment, these riches are prohibitively expensive and dangerous to exploit, but Royal Dutch Shell, ExxonMobil, and Scotland-based Cairn Energy are already betting on a lucrative future in the Arctic.[25] Among nations, Russia in particular has moved quickly to stake its claims. Moscow submitted an unsuccessful 2001 bid to the United Nations for sovereignty over 460,000 square miles of Arctic water, planted a flag at the North Pole in 2007, and is expected to submit another claim to the UN in 2012.[26] Other nations have submitted claims or are now preparing them, but again, in a G-Zero world, who will resolve such disputes?

In May 2011, the eight members of the Arctic Council reached their first and only decision concerning divisions of Arctic territory: They agreed on a treaty to organize burden sharing in search and rescue operations.[27] That's it. On issues of far greater international importance—the setting of boundaries that separate one country's claims from another's and both from international waters, the use of new sea lanes, and the exploitation of natural resources—the major players can't even agree to disagree. No substantial multilateral norms or regulations govern the Arctic. This is literally a new frontier.

Food Fights

Along with the air we breathe, the most basic of all necessities are food and water. Here's another fundamental G-Zero challenge:

With the most powerful economies less likely than at any time in decades to coordinate on a comprehensive solution to a complex problem, threats to "food security"—the availability of food and water at affordable prices—have never been more likely to stoke conflicts that destabilize entire societies. There is, and will continue to be, a global food market. But a variety of forces will generate food emergencies in coming years, and the lack of international leadership makes it highly unlikely that leading importers and exporters of food will agree to share the burdens of resolving them.

In 2007–2008, soaring prices for wheat, rice, corn, and soybeans—a phenomenon known as "agflation"—provoked a sharp spike in food prices and large-scale rioting in India, Pakistan, Egypt, Mexico, and several other countries.[28] By easing demand for grain, the financial crisis of late 2008 may have helped avert more severe food shortages. Yet as recovery from the market meltdown gathered steam, supply and demand factors again sent grain prices skyrocketing in early 2011, feeding the frustrations that generated upheaval across the Middle East and North Africa. A person who can't afford to eat has nothing to lose.

The forces adding to food costs are likely to grow stronger in years to come, and the G-Zero will make this issue much more difficult to manage. Global population growth drives food prices higher, but where people live and the kinds of food they eat matter more. The rise of middle classes inside emerging powers has moved hundreds of millions of people from a grain-based diet toward higher consumption of meat, a historical pattern repeated in every part of the world. A meat-based diet puts much more pressure on grain supplies than a grain-based diet because much more grain is needed to nourish livestock than to feed a human being.

That's why demand for grain will explode—unless we see a stunning reversal of surging economic growth rates in China, India, Brazil, Indonesia, and other emerging powers over the next several years. Even if higher prices lower demand for grain in America and Europe, China and India will more than make up the difference. In fact, China, already the world's second largest grain consumer, devoured 47 percent more corn in 2011 than in 2001, an increase that Brazil, the world's third largest grain producer, couldn't satisfy with its entire corn crop.[29]

The issue is not simply that demand is rising so quickly. On the supply side, urbanization across the emerging-market world adds to the price pressure by changing the ways in which both land and water are used. In 1950, just 29 percent of the world's population lived in cities. Today, it's more than 50 percent, a percentage that will rise for the foreseeable future as emerging countries continue to develop.[30] Most of this movement from the countryside into cities is taking place in China, India, Southeast Asia, and Africa. The McKinsey Global Institute forecasts that between 2012 and 2025, India's cities will take in another 215 million people, and China's cities will draw an additional 400 million.[31] With the sprawl of so many urban centers, the World Bank estimates that developing countries lose about 2.9 million hectares of cultivated farmland, an area larger than Massachusetts, every year.[32] That means a lot less farmland and a lot fewer farmers inside the countries with the world's fastest-growing demand for food. In addition, the urban poor are often first to face a food crisis—and the first to riot in response.

The second great pressure on food supplies comes from the drive to develop alternatives to hydrocarbon energy and the push for new biofuels—and the unwillingness of governments to agree on the threat this poses to food security. One day, governments will produce large quantities of biofuels from nonfood materials, but current technology limits development of most biofuel feedstocks to crops like corn and sugarcane for ethanol and oilseeds for biodiesel, diverting large numbers of crops from food to fuel. In the United States, 30 to 40 percent of the nation's corn crop now goes toward production of biofuels.

That's a key reason why Barack Obama and future U.S. presidents can't simply respond to a foreign famine as President Lyndon Johnson did in 1965 when he diverted one-fifth of America's wheat crop to feed the hungry in drought-ravaged India.[33] Large-scale diversion of corn toward biofuels helps ensure that America no longer has the crop surpluses or idle farmland to act as international food bank of last resort, and today's developing world has too many mouths to feed. The world's population hit seven billion in late 2011, with most of the gains coming in developing states.

The growth of biofuel production is not just an American phenomenon. The UN's Food and Agriculture Organization estimates that by 2020, 13 percent of the world's grain production, 15 percent of its vegetable oil, and 30 percent of its sugarcane will be used to make fuel.[34] Even a food crisis might not slow these plans. The United States, Brazil, and various European governments have invested too much money and political energy in these projects to sharply scale back production, and Indonesia, Japan, South Africa, and India are expanding their own biofuels programs. According to the International Energy Agency, 75 percent of the 2011 net growth in non-OPEC oil came from biofuels. Higher oil prices can exacerbate this issue in two ways. First, if crude oil prices spike, increased demand for biofuels will push grain prices higher too. Second, fertilizer production, irrigation, and food transport consume a lot of energy.

Estimates of the global impact of biofuels development on food supplies vary, but it's an obvious burden at a moment of steadily rising demand, and it will hit hardest in the world's poorest and most volatile countries. Grain price fluctuations tend to get lost in the average grocery bill in the United States, where so much food is highly processed and transportation and packaging account for a relatively large portion of the final price. But in developing countries, grain prices have a much bigger direct impact on the consumer because food is often consumed much closer to the place it was grown and because poorer people still spend more than half their income on food. This adds to the potential for riots and bloodshed that we've seen during localized food shocks in the recent past.

The inability to address climate change plays a role as well, because no factor is more important for food production than weather. The overwhelming scientific consensus is that rising global greenhouse gas emissions make droughts, floods, heat waves, and severe storms both more frequent and more damaging.[35] Poor harvests caused by higher temperatures, changes in rainfall levels, increased pollution, and the proliferation of weeds, pests, and disease in major food-producing regions have already contributed to higher food prices. In 2007 and 2008, droughts in Australia and Morocco and flooding in Argentina dealt major blows to wheat supplies, while rice crop infestation in Vietnam and freezing conditions in China took large amounts of rice off the market.

The ideal solution on food price security, as with so many other problems without borders, is to build an international system that promotes predictability and cooperation—or at the very least makes it much more difficult for individual states to hoard vital resources. In this case, negotiators could create a plan that helps lowest-cost producers grow crops and export them to countries that consume more than they grow. But food is the world's most politically sensitive commodity, and governments around the world have refused to work together on solutions that might come with a domestic political cost.

The largest G-Zero-related food issue is that the race to secure reliable supplies will empower producers at the expense of consumers—and encourage several forms of "food protectionism." We've seen this trend already. When grain and soybean prices tripled between 2007 and 2008, the governments of Russia and Argentina moved to keep local prices low and to safeguard domestic food supplies by restricting the export of wheat. Several grain exporters followed suit. Vietnam, a crucial source of rice for much of Southeast Asia, banned all rice exports for several months. The panicked governments of poor, import-dependent countries scrambled to cut side deals to secure access to grain supplies. Political officials in exporting countries, anxious to guard against shortages and unrest at home, weren't always willing to sell.[36]

To ensure that they aren't the countries left without supplies, China, South Korea, Saudi Arabia, and others have begun buying foreign land, particularly in Africa. In the process, they increase the risk of local unrest and regional conflict as hungry locals watch food grown next door loaded onto trucks for export to wealthier countries.[37] In Madagascar in 2008, public fury over a bid by South Korea's Daewoo Logistics to plant corn across a stretch of local land about half the size of Belgium helped topple a government.[38] Following a devastating drought in 2010, Russia, one of the world's largest grain producers, banned all exports of grain for several months. The move pushed prices sharply higher, deprived Russian farmers of opportunities to sell their crops abroad, and aggravated shortages in other parts of the world. Moscow's primary motive was to ensure that Russians had enough affordable food to avoid unrest during an election season, but the direct result was a deadly riot in Mozambique, one of Russia's out-of-luck customers.

Beyond export controls, governments of both established and emerging powers are now erecting import barriers to protect local farmers and food industries. In 2003, three infected cows set off a scare in the United States over mad cow disease, and the government of South Korea, a key U.S. ally, banned the import of U.S. beef, officially on health and safety grounds. The ban remained in place for five years. U.S. beef exporters complained that South Korea had simply seized an opportunity to protect its own beef industry. If conflicts like these are possible among reliable allies, imagine how countries might use these weapons against rivals, especially in the absence of viable international institutions to moderate disputes.

Whatever the motive, import barriers and heavy subsidies for local farmers reduce potential food supplies available to consumers and push prices higher. They also discourage the kinds of cross-border competition among producers that power technological advances to improve crop yields, increase supplies, and make food more affordable. The Doha Round of World Trade Organization talks is now lying by the side of the road awaiting a decent burial in part because U.S. and European negotiators have refused to ask their farmers to compete on a level playing field.

Food security is a classic G-Zero question, because there is no consensus international strategy on what to do when rising food prices create a crisis—or on how to prevent these crises before they happen. The United States remains the lead donor for the UN World Food Program, but given that organization's limited means and mandate, it can do little more than respond to local emergencies.

In preparation for a special session of the UN's Food and Agriculture Organization in Rome in September 2011, economist Abdolreza Abbassian promised to pose every government delegate in attendance a simple question: "Are you preparing yourself for food security?"[39] But that is exactly the wrong question. Individual governments have already developed dozens of ways to protect their own populations. Here's the real question: Can the leaders of both exporting and importing nations agree to accept the shared risks, costs, and sacrifices needed for a global solution to meet a global challenge? In a G-Zero world, the answer is no.

Water

Water covers about 70 percent of the earth's surface, but only about 2.5 percent of that total is freshwater, and most of that is frozen in ice caps. As a result, only about 0.007 percent of the world's water is available for human use.[40] It was this scarcity that led then–World Bank vice president Ismail Serageldin to warn in 1995 that "the wars of the next century will be about water."[41] Former UN secretary-general Kofi Annan repeated this warning as the new century dawned.[42] The fear is entirely plausible: Population growth and industrialization have sharply increased global demand for water that is often shared across national boundaries. At least 263 water basins around the world are divided between two or more countries.[43] The 1997 UN Convention on the Law of the Non-Navigational Uses of International Watercourses[44] called for "equitable and reasonable use" of shared water systems and prohibits one country from using water access to impose "significant harm" on another state. Just sixteen states have agreed to abide by its rules.

An every-nation-for-itself approach to water contributes to food security problems—and creates risks of its own. Countries like Japan and Saudi Arabia that don't have enough farmland to meet domestic demand for food have poured too much money and far too much water into inefficient and expensive local production of grains. In the Middle East, northern and eastern Africa, and South Asia, in particular, freshwater has become an increasingly scarce resource. Urbanization, pollution, and climate change are adding to the stresses. The amount of water needed for crops varies a lot from place to place and crop to crop, but 70 percent of the world's freshwater is used for agriculture, and the production of meat demands six to twenty times more water than grain production does.[45] In the United States, production of one pound of beef requires more than 370 gallons of water.

The most efficient market-driven government method of guarding against shortages of a vital resource is to increase the price that consumers pay for it. Yet in countries all over the world, both established and emerging, citizens believe they have a right to clean water, and efforts to protect supplies by inflating their price often provoke outrage—and sometimes violence. Given that water is essential for production of the world's food, local water supplies are everyone's concern. In a G-Zero world, it will be ever more difficult to persuade governments to cooperate on plans that impose locally unpopular policies for the global public good.

Potential water conflict zones are many, but the most worrisome are in Asia and Africa. First, the world's two most populous countries, India and China, already face serious questions on water security as climate change, industrialization, and the growth of cities in both countries make unprecedented demands on access to clean water. China is the world's "unrivaled hydro-hegemon."[46] More freshwater flowing across international borders comes from China than from any other country. Not coincidentally, China has built more dams, including the world's largest (Three Gorges), than every other country in the world combined, an issue that threatens the water supplies of India, Bangladesh, Thailand, Laos, Vietnam, Cambodia, and Russia—all of which have issued formal complaints. China is also fast becoming a leading exporter of dam-related technology, allowing other governments to exacerbate the problem by gaining the means to hoard more water within their borders.

Then there is the challenge in Africa. The world's longest river, the Nile, is sourced from three rivers—the Blue Nile, the White Nile, and the Atbara—and flows north through a total of twelve countries. The Nile basin is now home to about 370 million people, a number that continues to grow. Climate change is heating things up. Recurring droughts have already killed or displaced millions in Sudan, Ethiopia, and Kenya over the years, and conflicts driven by competition over water, food, and land are increasingly likely to trigger large-scale violence.

Egypt, the country farthest downstream, relies on the Nile for 90 percent of its water supply.[47] Harnessing the Nile with the construction of dams and a complex irrigation system, Egypt has used hydroelectricity generation and agriculture to fuel its economy and feed its people. Upstream countries continue to observe a 1959 agreement between Egypt and Sudan that allows Egypt to receive the majority of the Nile's water. But in May 2010, Ethiopia (leader of the upstream countries), Rwanda, Tanzania, Uganda, and Kenya signed the Cooperative Framework Agreement, which, if ratified, would strip Egypt of the rights granted it in 1959 and create the Nile Basin Commission to manage water sharing. Burundi signed the CFA in February 2011, and the Democratic Republic of Congo plans to sign on soon. To defend its rights, Egypt has adopted a strategy of negotiating individually with upstream countries, offering help with water development plans in exchange for pledges not to void the 1959 treaty.

In the meantime, water shortages persist, and upstream nations face resource pressures they can't ignore. In April 2011, Ethiopia began construction of one large-scale dam project, with plans for two more. Uganda broke ground on a dam and is pursuing a water management program in the Lake Victoria basin with Burundi, Kenya, Tanzania, and Rwanda. As each country looks to defend its supplies, the risk of conflict grows. In a region that has seen so much strife over the decades, this is the greatest underreported danger.

*　*　*

G-Zero crises echo and exacerbate one another. A lack of global leadership makes it all but impossible to build consensus on what to do about climate change, droughts, floods, and the food price shocks they trigger. State efforts to manage the fallout breed protectionism, which slows growth and poisons international relationships, and gives governments new incentives to hoard information and control communications. This generates more public anger, more turmoil, and more G-Zero. Fundamental reforms that reorder entire societies, frictions among powerful states, intensifying competition in the world's most volatile regions, shortages of food and water, and devastating cyberattacks on a country's nerve center all produce fear that undermines the chance for collaborative leadership. The greatest risk of all is that what begins in fear will end in folly.

In short, the G-Zero will incubate new sources of conflict, make almost all of them more difficult to manage, and push international politics toward multiple forms of crisis. But for every risk there's an opportunity. For every loser there's a winner. The G-Zero will produce plenty of both, and that's the subject of the next chapter.

CHAPTER FOUR

Winners and Losers

There is no security on this earth, there is only opportunity.
—General Douglas MacArthur

Few countries on earth are as vulnerable to rising tides as the Republic of Maldives, a string of 1,190 coral islands stretching north–south a few hundred miles from India's southwest coast. About 80 percent of its islands are less than forty inches above sea level, and the UN's Intergovernmental Panel on Climate Change has warned that unless global warming is reversed, the Indian Ocean could rise to swallow the Maldives by the end of this century.[1] That's why, even before he arrived in Copenhagen for the ill-fated global climate summit, President

Mohamed Nasheed decided on a dramatic play for the world's attention.

On October 17, 2009, Nasheed convened the most unusual cabinet meeting in history. Once security officials had checked a nearby reef for signs of dangerous sea creatures, the Maldives' first democratically elected president and eleven of his fourteen ministers donned scuba gear and dropped into a crystal-clear turquoise lagoon off Girifushi, an island used mainly for local military exercises. Sixteen feet below the surface, Nasheed and his cabinet began the meeting around a horseshoe-shaped table anchored on the seabed. Before an audience of awkwardly snorkeling journalists, several schools of parrotfish, and at least one stingray, the twelve men used whiteboards and hand signals to approve a document that called on all nations to reduce the carbon emissions that many scientists warn are heating up the atmosphere, melting polar ice caps, and raising sea levels around the world. The event lasted about thirty minutes.

Asked later to outline his hopes for the upcoming meeting in Copenhagen, Nasheed said simply, "We hope not to die."[2] But without leaders willing and able to enforce the compromises needed to resolve a transnational challenge like climate change, the Maldives will one day slip beneath the waves.

The G-Zero won't bring bad news for everyone. Like Western-led globalization or the U.S.-dominated single-superpower world, the G-Zero will produce both winners and losers across a broad range of countries, companies, and organizations. Plenty of books and articles in recent years have staked out positions in the great debate over globalization and its impact. Some say it has done enormous good around the world, particularly in developing countries, by lifting hundreds of millions of new workers and consumers into the global economy and connecting them in ever more complex networks of trade.[3] Others say globalization has inflicted enormous harm by empowering large corporations at the expense of ordinary people or by moving jobs from the leading industrialized economies toward countries where workers accept lower wages.[4] Globalization has been a lot better for Bangalore and New York than for Yekaterinburg, Russia, and Youngstown, Ohio.

The same pro and con arguments have been made about America's role as the world's only superpower. Some say that recklessness from Washington to Wall Street has unleashed wars and financial chaos around the globe. Others insist that the sheer scale of American consumption allows the United States to import huge volumes of products from emerging-market states, creating millions of jobs and lifting developing countries to new heights. American drone attacks provoke rage in Pakistan and Afghanistan, and some influential Afghani political leaders are pushing hard for the last U.S. troops to leave their country. Yet the American military presence in some of the world's most dangerous regions keeps commerce moving and maintains an often delicate balance of power. From that angle, without America, there is no rise of the rest.

Both these generalizations reflect elements of truth. Globalization and American hegemony are neither inherently good nor inherently evil. They have boosted some and sunk others. So it is with the G-Zero: In general, it will create a more challenging economic environment, but some governments, institutions, companies, and individuals will be adaptable enough to thrive in a leaderless world. Others will not.

A WORLD IN FLUX

A world without leadership will provoke a fundamental reordering of international politics. Let's start with the Middle East. In May 2011, President Barack Obama announced what U.S. officials described as a "reset" of U.S. policy in the region, a new beginning for a formula that was no longer viable. Obama clearly likes the symbolism of dropping off the baggage and restarting relationships with a clean slate. His first major foreign policy initiative was a reset of U.S. relations with Russia following years of growing mistrust and animosity. But here's the difference: Obama's Russia reset was proactive, a product of careful planning, while that with the Arab world was a hurriedly devised reaction to unforeseen regional upheaval.

An uprising in Tunisia, revolution in Egypt, rage in Bahrain, chaos in Yemen, bloodshed in Syria, and civil war in Libya left U.S. policymakers scrambling for a plan to keep Washington relevant to fast-moving events—with strategies that recognized each country, conflict, and relationship as unique. The move did little to ease the uncertainty over the shifting balance of power and allegiances in the Arab world. U.S. support for protests in Egypt taught the Saudis that they might not be able to count on Washington if similar unrest were to swell in Riyadh—and a more cautious U.S. approach to an uprising in Bahrain that pitted majority Shia demonstrators against a Sunni monarch did not change their minds. It's no longer clear that the American president and Saudi princes speak the same political language.

Aware that U.S. influence in the region is on the wane, the Saudis are now investing more hope and resources in the Gulf Cooperation Council, an organization formed in the wake of the 1979 Iranian revolution to pool the power of Gulf Arab states, contain

Tehran's bid for greater regional influence, and integrate the Persian Gulf economies. In 2011, the GCC intervened in Bahrain to put down demands for reform from local Shia. It also formally invited Jordan and Morocco, the Arab world's other large monarchies, to join the club.[5] The Arab world's upheaval has produced another major change. Egypt has now awakened from a generational slumber to again play a leading role in the region—and with new approaches to old problems. It's not yet clear how Egypt's new government will treat relations with Israel, though it will almost certainly be more responsive to Egyptian public opinion than was the Mubarak regime. That's a significant new wild card for the entire Middle East.

Yes, a reset *is* under way in the Arab world, but this one creates less space, not more, for the United States. In Washington, Republicans and Democrats spent most of 2011 arguing over how far and how fast to slash government spending. With U.S. troops still involved in Iraq and Afghanistan and American forces contributing to the NATO pummeling of Libya's Muammar Gadhafi, Washington had little appetite for becoming more deeply implicated in the Arab world's turmoil. Instead, the Obama administration was left to try to sell the idea of "leading from behind," a formula that allows Washington to use its still singular military power to buttress efforts led by others. The phrase makes political advisors cringe, but it may well reflect a more effective use of U.S. military power at a historical moment that demands modesty and austerity.[*]

Aware of Washington's new limits, major Middle East players

---

[*] The phrase did not actually come from Obama. It was attributed to an unnamed administration official who was describing the president's approach to Gadhafi's Libya. As Ryan Lizza, the journalist who published the "leading from behind" comment in the *New Yorker,* has acknowledged, the concept was first championed years ago by Nelson Mandela. Ryan Lizza, "Leading from Behind," *New Yorker,* April 27, 2011, http://www.newyorker.com/online/blogs/newsdesk/2011/04/leading-from-behind-obama-clinton.html.

know they can no longer count on the United States to backstop regional stability. America has become dangerously overextended in recent years, and the region's heavyweights will be forced to deepen ties with other trade and investment partners. For example, to ensure that demands for change in neighboring Bahrain and Yemen don't encourage young Saudis to challenge the House of Saud's right to rule, King Abdullah announced in spring 2011 that his government would spend hundreds of billions of dollars on projects intended to bolster stability, from construction of new houses and subsidies for new mortgages to the training of more security troops and payoffs to politically loyal religious authorities.[6] To ensure a steady stream of revenue, the Saudis will also have to sell more oil, making energy-thirsty China a useful strategic partner. The royals know they needn't worry that Beijing will suddenly support a popular Arab uprising, and in exchange for access to Saudi oil, China can contribute to the infrastructure projects that improve quality of life for millions of Saudi citizens. Of course, the Saudis will continue selling oil to America, Europe, and others able to pay, but the days when senior U.S. and Saudi officials could resolve serious problems with a few private conversations are probably over. This is a seismic shift in the political landscape of the Middle East.

As we saw in the previous chapter, Asia is becoming the most potentially unstable region in the world. In East and Southeast Asia, many governments still rely on the United States to provide a counterweight to China's rise, but Washington's more limited means will raise new doubts there as well about American staying power. These doubts are as prevalent in Japan, Taiwan, and South Korea as in Thailand, the Philippines, Indonesia, and Vietnam. As Kishore Mahbubani, a former permanent secretary of Singapore's Foreign ministry, once said, Asians "know that China will still be in Asia in 1,000 years' time, but don't know whether America will still be here in 100 years' time."[7] Or perhaps in ten years' time. Meanwhile, U.S. relations with Pakistan are increasingly under fire inside both countries. Decidedly mixed feelings about America at every level of Pakistani society may push a vulnerable civilian government to turn toward China as an ally against rival India and as a primary source of cash should Washington follow through on threats to reduce aid.

WINNERS

Who wins and who loses in this exceptionally fluid international environment? A winner is made more prosperous and secure by a world without leadership, and has more options and greater influence than it had before. Winners have choices. A loser is one made less prosperous, secure, and influential because it has fewer political and commercial avenues to explore. The first key to surviving and thriving in this period of transition is to recognize that changes to the global system will enable an unprecedented number of governments to play by their own rules. Those who still operate as if borders are opening, barriers are falling, the world is becoming a single market, and the president of the United States is "leader of the free world" will find themselves reacting to events that they don't understand.

Pivot States

With few enforceable international rules and regulations, some regional heavyweights will find a wealth of new opportunities. Take Brazil, now the world's eighth largest economy and a state with many important advantages. Brazil lives in one of the world's safest neighborhoods. Corruption and organized crime remain chronic problems in Latin America, but the risk of traditional military conflict there is much lower than in any other part of the emerging-market world. There are no battles over nuclear weapons proliferation. Terrorism and militancy remain local problems in a few states.

Brazil is also home to the region's largest consumer market. The country's middle class now numbers more than 100 million people, with millions more emerging from poverty over the next several years. Brazil profited mightily by embracing globalization and is now responsible for about 40 percent of the region's GDP.[8] Its government, led for the last decade by a party of the left, has helped establish a consensus across the domestic political spectrum in favor of a policy emphasis on low inflation and openness to foreign investment in most sectors. Its economy is well diversified. Brazil is already self-sufficient in energy, and huge offshore oil discoveries in 2007 ensure that the country will soon become one of the world's largest oil exporters. It was able to rebound quickly from the financial crisis and global slowdown. In a G-Zero world, Brazil can compete with the United States as both a source of and a destination for regional wealth and investment.

Another factor makes Brazil a winner: It has built strong political ties and promising commercial relations with the United States, China, and a growing number of other emerging-market countries. For eighty years, the United States was Brazil's largest trade partner. Commerce between them remains substantial and will continue to benefit both. But during the first decade of the twenty-first century, Brazil's imports from China rose twelvefold and its exports to China jumped eighteenfold.[9] In early 2009, China replaced the United States as Brazil's largest trade partner. In the process, Brazil has become a *pivot state,* a country able to build profitable relationships with multiple other countries without becoming overly reliant on any one of them. Over the past thirty years, international winners were those states that adapted to and profited from the processes of Western-led globalization. In a world with regional centers of gravity, one in which no country plays the global leader, governments must create more of their own opportunities. The ability to pivot is a critical advantage.

Turkey has built a similar position. Its bid to join the European Union is going nowhere—a veto from any single EU member can keep an applicant out, and several of them don't want an expanded union that borders Iran, Iraq, and Syria. Yet Turkey is actively expanding its international influence. NATO membership already gives Ankara a voice in the United States and in Europe, and the country is also an increasingly important global market, with per capita income nearly double that of China and four times that of India. Many in the Arab world look to Turkey as a dynamic, modern Muslim state, with an economy four times the size of Egypt's despite having virtually the same population. Though traditional ties with Israel have become severely strained in recent years, Turkey still enjoys deeper trade relations with its government than does any other country in the Muslim world.[10] Turkey has developed the geopolitical self-confidence to run ambitious foreign policy initiatives over the objections of the world's most powerful governments, and its position at the crossroads of Europe, Asia, the Middle East, and the former Soviet Union make it the very model of a pivot state.

In some ways, Africa has become a pivot continent. Thanks to its reputation for chronic poverty, corruption, conflict, and disease, it remains the world's most underrated growth story. Between 2000 and 2010, its real GDP grew at 4.7 percent per year, double the rate of the 1980s and 1990s—though turmoil in Egypt and the shutdown of Libya's oil exports slowed things a bit in 2011. Africa's population surpassed one billion people in 2010, roughly equal to India's, but Africans spent 35 percent more on goods and services in 2008 than Indians did. The percentage of Africans who live in cities is now comparable to China and greater than India. In the first decade of this century, more than 320 million Africans signed up for mobile phones. Total foreign direct investment in the continent grew from $9.4 billion in 2000 to $46.4 billion in 2009. In addition, though many think of Africa's wealth primarily in terms of oil and metals production, urbanization across the continent and growing middle classes in many countries ensure that African economies that don't export huge quantities of commodities have grown almost as fast as those that do.[11]

Africa has achieved this success in part because many of its governments can now pivot. For many years, cash-strapped African states had to turn almost exclusively to the IMF, the World Bank, and Western governments for the aid and investment they needed to fund development. They accepted this flow of Western money with reluctance in some cases, because the money often came with strings attached— such as demands for greater openness to Western investment and for democratic reforms. The funding also stoked anger among ordinary citizens because it too often went directly to chronically corrupt governments, with little trickling down to local people.

Yet over the past decade—just as in Brazil and other parts of the emerging-market world—China has sharply increased its investment in the region. To gain long-term access to oil, gas, metals, minerals, and farmland in Africa, the state-backed China Development Bank and the Export-Import Bank of China have become major investors in the continent. In 2010 alone, China's trade with Africa expanded by more than 43 percent, according to official Chinese trade data, enough to allow China to replace the United States as Africa's largest trade partner. In response, U.S. officials have insisted that China must observe international standards—those established by Western negotiators—which demand transparency, compliance with procurement rules, and other concessions that allow for a "level competitive playing field" and "generate maximum benefits for [African] countries and their citizens."[12] But Washington can do virtually nothing to enforce these rules. Nongovernmental organizations and high-profile individuals are left to fight their own battles. For example, American film director Steven Spielberg managed to embarrass the Chinese by resigning from an advisory post for the 2008 Beijing Olympic Games to protest Chinese support for Sudan's government.

The story here is not that China wins and America loses, because the investment picture isn't nearly that simple. The real winner is Africa, which can now expect multinational and state-owned companies from the established and emerging-market worlds to compete for access to African consumers and favorable investment terms. Chinese companies have made much of their headway in Africa by bankrolling large infrastructure projects and by ensuring that local people, not just grasping bureaucrats, reap the rewards. Yet they've also insisted in many cases that a large percentage of the materials used in these projects come from China, and that roads, bridges, port facilities, and airports be built by Chinese workers, who often remain in Africa after the projects are complete. The presence of these foreign workers has already aroused anger in several African countries, where Chinese labor deprives locals of jobs. In September 2011, Michael Sata, an outspoken critic of China's role in Africa, was elected president of Zambia. There is no reason why Western-based companies can't exploit these vulnerabilities and compete more effectively with Chinese companies.

Still, China and other emerging markets do seem quicker than the United States to recognize the value of closer ties with Africa and the possibilities that the G-Zero can create. That's one big reason why the BRIC countries invited South Africa to join their club in December 2010. By traditional measures, South Africa's economy can't begin to compete with those of the other BRICs (Brazil, Russia, India, and China). The IMF estimated in 2010 that it was less than one-quarter the size of Russia's, the smallest of the four BRICs, and just 6 percent of China's.[13] But South Africa is a member of the Southern African Development Community, a collection of emerging states that includes Angola, Africa's second largest oil producer; Botswana, the world's largest diamond producer; Zambia, the continent's biggest copper producer; and Mozambique, with enormous untapped reserves of coal. Building a bridge to Africa opens enormous opportunities for some of the world's fastest-growing emerging-market players, and the bridge enriches partners on both sides. That's the power of the pivot.[14]

Given that Asia will be the biggest contributor to global economic growth over the next many years, it's not surprising that the region is home to several pivot states. Indonesia, with the world's fourth largest population, has enjoyed a stable political environment in recent years with solid GDP growth. Its natural resources and relative openness to foreign investment attract customers from around the world, but Indonesia's is also a well-diversified economy that benefits from a highly skilled workforce, a fast-growing middle class, a strong educational system, an expanding manufacturing base, and a surge in tourism revenue. More than half of Indonesians are under thirty years old, allowing growth to continue on a solid base for many years without the aging population that will impose enormous financial burdens and policy challenges for Europe, China, and Japan. Indonesia is a classic pivot state because its trade ties are well balanced among China, the United States, Japan, and Singapore— and are likely to remain so.

Vietnam, too, can pivot because it receives most of its development aid from Japan, its arms from Russia, its machinery (and tourists) from China, and its biggest export market from the United States. Vietnam began its economic reform process several years later than China, but by 1986, the Doi Moi (renovation) process was well under way. Real GDP growth has averaged about 7.5 percent over the past twenty years, and the poverty rate fell from 58 percent in 1993 to just 14.5 percent in 2008.[15] China could eventually dominate its much smaller neighbor, but for now, Vietnam profits from a diverse set of partners.

A country's small size doesn't always limit its government's geopolitical options, as tiny Singapore demonstrates. With centuries of experience as a trading hub, the island city-state—it is about the size of Lexington, Kentucky, and has a population of five million people—sits at the mouth of the Strait of Malacca, through which one-third of the world's seaborne traffic passes every day. Singapore's per capita GDP is among the highest in the world, while unemployment hovers at about 2 percent. Since independence in 1965, Singapore has had just three prime ministers, all from the People's Action Party, creating an elite that governs largely by consensus. No entrenched domestic interests fearful of foreign competition have the leverage to sway government policy, and the island remains open to outside investment. Aware of these advantages, Singapore's government has worked to marry Eastern culture and Western business practices, and the country is now the world's fourth leading financial center, behind London, New York, and Hong Kong. In a G-Zero environment, there are too many major players in Asia for any one country, even China, to fully dominate Asia. Many foreign companies looking to set up shop there want a base that allows them access to all of Asia's power economies without overreliance on any of them, and Singapore has done very well by offering many of those companies a home. China, India, Indonesia, and the United States all have good reasons to do business there.

In Central Asia, resource-rich Mongolia understands the need to pivot. To escape the competing gravitational pulls of China and Russia, its government has adopted a "third neighbor" policy, a bid to form better commercial relations with the United States and with other Asian countries. Also wedged between Russia and China, Kazakhstan is already profiting from its position as a pivot state. This former Soviet republic has developed one of the world's fastest-growing economies, thanks mainly to the large-scale export of oil, metals, and grains that helps ensure it doesn't rely too heavily for trade on Russia, its former Soviet partner, or on China. Almaty, the country's largest city, has become an important regional financial center. Though Kazakhstan takes part in a customs union with Russia and is a member of the Shanghai Cooperation Organization, a security pact that includes both Russia and China, its largest trade partner is the European Union. Indeed, Kazakhstan exports almost as much to Germany as to either of its powerful neighbors.

Not all pivot states are emerging markets. Canada remains vulnerable to a slowdown in the United States, though not as vulnerable as it used to be—and not nearly as exposed as Mexico. Thanks to the financial crisis and its impact on American purchasing power, the percentage of Canada's exports to countries other than the United States jumped from 18 percent in 2005 to more than 25 percent just four years later. Canada now draws nearly 40 percent of its imports from countries other than its giant neighbor to the south.[16] This trend is not simply the product of the global market meltdown; Canada was working to build commercial ties with Asia for years before the recession took hold in the United States and is now well on its way to finishing a free trade agreement with the European Union.

Rogues with Powerful Friends

When established powers want to pressure smaller states to change their behavior, they're more likely than ever to resort to sanctions—economic and diplomatic penalties that provide a relatively low-cost, low-risk alternative to military action. We've seen that with efforts to isolate governments like Iran, North Korea, Myanmar, and Syria. But in a G-Zero world, sanctions will be even less effective than they've been in the past. First, the threat of military action that might produce unforeseen consequences is a crucial tool for building support for sanctions. War fatigue in the United States and fiscal austerity in Europe make that threat less credible. Second, in a world where Washington holds less of the political and economic leverage necessary for effective diplomatic arm-twisting, other states will be less willing to impose sanctions that undermine their own commercial interests.

That's why *rogues with powerful friends,* states that openly flout international rules with cover from other governments, will profit from the lack of a strong referee to enforce them. Successful testing of a nuclear device has given North Korea a kind of international "get out of jail free" card, one that its government plays whenever it wants to draw concessions from China, South Korea, and others by raising alert levels on and around the Korean Peninsula. Washington continues to take a hard line on negotiations with Pyongyang, and sanctions have targeted the assets of the leadership itself, inflicting personal pain on senior officials. But China's fear of chaos across its northeastern border provides North Korea with enough cash, food, fuel, and diplomatic cover to resist foreign pressure.

Four thousand miles to the west, Iran's leaders had a ringside seat for the U.S. assault on Saddam Hussein in 2003. They recognized that Saddam's inability to develop a nuclear weapon denied him the shield that continues to protect the government in North Korea. That's one reason why Iran has pushed full speed ahead with development of a weapons capability—and why it will probably one day cross the nuclear finish line. Between now and then, Iran will have to cope with a variety of international sanctions on the export of nuclear materials, missiles, and other military matériel; investment in oil, gas, and petrochemicals; and shipping, banking, and insurance transactions. The purpose of these sanctions is not simply to slow or halt Iran's uranium enrichment program; it's also to ensure that the next wave of would-be weapons states can see just how dangerous and expensive nuclear development in violation of international agreements can be. But too many governments are interested in Iran's oil and gas to maintain effective sanctions on its energy trade.

In Myanmar, an authoritarian military regime suppresses domestic demand for democracy and brutalizes and jails civilian protesters. Fortunately for the ruling junta, China, India, and others want continued access to Myanmar's substantial deposits of natural gas, and China has built a major new oil and gas pipeline linking the two countries. With active diplomatic support for "noninterference" in Myanmar's "internal affairs," Vietnam helps its government deflect international criticism and ensure that democracy and human rights don't become requirements for membership in the Association of Southeast Asian Nations, a regional grouping that includes both states as members. Thailand is building a highway from Bangkok to Myanmar's west coast to ease the shipment of goods to South Asia.*

---

* In late 2011, Myanmar showed signs of trying to become a pivot state. Political concessions and a shift in rhetoric earned a visit from Secretary of State Hillary Clinton. It remains to be seen if Myanmar will follow through, but even Myanmar's leaders recognize that a single powerful friend can't beat the power of the pivot.

There's nothing new about North Korea, Iran, and Myanmar flouting international rules with support from powerful friends, but over the years, sanctions have done serious damage to all three. As more governments become self-confident enough to resist rules foisted on them by outsiders, and as it becomes more obvious that there is no country or bloc of countries with the leverage to enforce these rules, virtually all forms of sanction will become more difficult to impose and enforce. With every nation for itself, the next wave of would-be nuclear powers will see that—and may decide that they too can safely ignore demands from established powers.

COMPANIES AND THE COMPETITIVE EDGE

The G-Zero will provide many different kinds of companies and institutions with important advantages. First, well-managed and well-positioned state-owned enterprises, politically loyal national champions, favored banks, and sovereign wealth funds will continue to profit from the competitive boost their governments can provide them. Stories of Chinese and Russian policymakers finding creative ways to tip the commercial playing field to favor their favorites, both at home and abroad, have become well known, but we're also seeing this trend in emerging-market democracies. Brazil's government has passed a series of laws that make state-owned oil company Petrobras the lead operator for new exploration and production activity involving the country's massive offshore oil deposits. The legislation is also designed to develop a local oil service industry by requiring that set percentages of equipment and services used to produce all that new oil come from Brazilian suppliers.[17]

Given the scale and complexity involved in drawing so much oil from so deep beneath the seabed, and the fact that Petrobras already has its hands full with existing projects, it's possible that the company will be asked to do more than it's capable of. Perhaps these rigid rules will make for a bigger, less efficient national oil company, and the arrival of major new oil supplies on the market, which could help lower prices, will be needlessly delayed. But it's also possible that commercial relationships with select foreign companies, including Chinese and other state-owned firms, will give Petrobras a good opportunity to broaden its capabilities while learning from the expertise and experience of others. That's a winning formula.

Adapters

Among multinational companies, it's the *adapters* that will be most successful—those that understand the changing competitive landscape and are agile enough to exploit the advantages it provides. As Charles Darwin once noted, it isn't the strongest or the smartest who survive; it's the ones most capable of change. Some companies can respond to a world with fewer enforceable rules by exploiting arbitrage opportunities to minimize tax and regulatory burdens. When German taxpayers were asked to bankroll a rescue package for Ireland and its failing banks in 2010, German lawmakers griped that the Irish government should raise corporate taxes to bring them into line with the rates demanded in Germany. On the surface, that's an entirely reasonable demand. Arguably, Ireland's government might not have found itself strapped for cash had it not tried to attract business and investment by offering foreign companies advantages that Germany did not. But Ireland knows that if it doesn't offer these incentives, some multinationals operating within its borders will simply relocate, perhaps to countries outside the European Union, in search of lower taxes. Just as many American companies have shifted jobs overseas to take advantage of lower-cost labor in developing countries, so a growing number of Chinese firms have moved operations to take advantage of cheap labor in Southeast Asia. In short, companies adaptable enough to move toward the best deal will profit most. More banks, hedge funds, and private equity funds will shift their operations toward emerging-market states to avoid global and Western regulatory reforms. Some banks will adapt much more quickly than others to rule changes within individual countries. The G-Zero ensures that there will be many more such opportunities.

Another form of adapter is the multinational that can transform a state-backed rival into a commercial partner by offering something that a government-controlled enterprise can't get anywhere else, like access to battle-tested advanced technology or services that demand unique expertise. A number of multinational oil firms now spend less time and money on exploration and production and more on providing services that help state-owned companies operate more efficiently.

British Petroleum has partnered with China National Petroleum Corporation to extract and sell oil produced in Iraq. Exxon-Mobil has partnered with Rosneft, Russia's largest oil producer, to develop Russian offshore oilfields in the Arctic. Rosneft gains exposure to state-of-the-art deep-sea drilling technology and expertise, probably including projects in the United States. For its part, ExxonMobil will win a share of one of the world's last untapped resource-rich regions.

But opportunities extend far beyond the energy sector. Companies like Japan's Kawasaki, Germany's Siemens, France's Alstom, and Canada's Bombardier have partnered with Chinese firms on lucrative joint projects to build high-speed train systems. There is a catch: These foreign firms have had many of their designs appropriated by their Chinese partners and now find themselves competing with those companies inside China and in other countries such as Brazil and Saudi Arabia.[18] That's why it's not enough to invest in partnerships. These companies must invest in a culture of adaptability.

To respond to changing circumstances within fast-evolving markets, adaptability often takes the form of diversification. Few companies in the world are as adaptable as India's Tata Group. It is Asia's largest software exporter. It's also one of the world's top ten producers of commercial vehicles, the world's largest tea producer, and the sixth largest watch manufacturer. It operates a chain of luxury hotels, and is India's largest private-sector power utility. Profitable joint ventures may boost profits this year and next, but rules change quickly in a G-Zero environment, and multinational companies should accept the need to follow Tata's lead and search out new opportunities. Adaptability is not one-size-fits-all. While it can pay to be small, in the G-Zero, specialization can be dangerous. Some of the conglomerates once disparaged as lumbering and inefficient can now keep eggs in many baskets, standing to gain accordingly.

Protectors
Then there are those who find ways to take advantage of every nation for itself—the *protectors* and the *cheaters*. Protectors—firms involved in defense against conventional military strikes, cyber-attacks, terrorism, or commercial piracy—will prosper in a G-Zero world, particularly if they're able to align themselves with deep-pocketed governments. The G-Zero is a period of great transition, and significant changes in the international balance of power stoke both competition among would-be regional powers and anxiety among those who fear they aren't yet ready to compete. Whether the competition involves the kind of posturing we've seen in the

South China Sea—as China, Taiwan, Vietnam, South Korea, the Philippines, and others stake claims to disputed territory—or the risk of cyberattack from states looking to frustrate potential rivals at minimum cost, companies that offer governments new offensive and defensive capabilities will find lots of new opportunities.

In addition, as some traditional U.S. allies begin to question Washington's long-term commitment to guarantee their security, both local and foreign defense contractors (and the companies with whom they partner) will win new business. The economic sectors that profit most from the G-Zero include defense contractors working with countries that can afford to boost military spending (like India), those that see the G-Zero environment as an opportunity to extend their regional influence (like China), and those that fear they may be less able to rely on outside actors to safeguard their security (like Japan, South Korea, and Israel). But U.S. defense contractors especially will also find themselves competing in a marketplace filled with customers ready to flex their own muscles and less respectful of America's global sway. Witness China's threats to punish Boeing, Lockheed Martin, Raytheon, and others for their part in a $6.4 billion arms deal with Taiwan. The old logic was that China couldn't sanction Boeing and others without undermining its own aviation industry. In a leaderless world, China might be ready to assume that risk.

There are other forms of security and other forms of protectors. China needs more clean freshwater each year. According to the Asia Water Project, a business research organization, China's demand for water will grow 63 percent by 2030.[19] That's why State Development & Investment Corporation (SDIC), a Chinese state-owned investment holding company, has invested billions in the Beijiang Power and Desalination Plant, a facility well on its way to becoming China's largest source of desalted water. This plant was built almost entirely in Israel before being shipped to northeastern China for assembly. But in years to come, the National Development and Reform Commission, China's central state planning agency, will favor Chinese desalination companies with more investment, tax cuts, and low-interest loans. Beijing's goal is to finance development of a Chinese desalination industry, first to meet local demand for freshwater, and eventually to become a world leader in freshwater technology.[20] This new industry will protect China's water security. Water security, in turn, will protect the Chinese Communist Party's monopoly hold on political power, and the Chinese government will thus protect the industry—another virtuous circle kept strong by mutual self-interest.

Cheaters

In a G-Zero world, *cheaters* will prosper. The G-Zero is not a world without rules, but when no one has the means to enforce them, they will be much easier to manipulate or ignore. Within the G20, no deal will be agreed on and enforced unless all major players want it to succeed. That's an impossibly high bar for almost any substantive plan and has the potential to stymie everything from agreements on new rules and standards for trade and coordination of tax policies to efforts to stimulate global growth, avoid currency wars, and achieve a meaningful agreement on climate change. Even when an agreement is ratified, those who sign on can safely ignore it whenever they choose, since no one has the muscle to penalize them for it.

Companies from all over the world are looking to profit from access to commodities in Africa, but some players in the new game, particularly those from Western countries, still have to play by the old rules. For many years, in states like the Democratic Republic of Congo, Sierra Leone, Côte d'Ivoire, and Zimbabwe, insurgents and local governments have sold diamonds to finance wars or government repression, earning the gems the epithet "blood diamonds."

In 1998, the South African government hosted a meeting in the town of Kimberley that brought together officials from diamond-trading and -producing states, several rights groups, and representatives of the diamond industry to find a solution to the blood diamond problem. Three years of tough negotiations produced the Kimberley Process (KP), an international diamond certification system endorsed in January 2003 by the United Nations, which requires governments of countries that produce or trade diamonds to certify where they come from. Member states have to create local laws and regulations that keep blood diamonds off the market and can only trade uncut diamonds with other KP members, giving governments a powerful incentive to join the club. So far, seventy-five governments have signed on.[21] But this is one of the many international agreements unlikely to generate even modest success in a G-Zero world.

In June 2011, for instance, President Robert Mugabe of Zimbabwe announced that his cash-starved government would ignore international agreements to sell diamonds from its controversial Marange mine, which Zimbabwe claims could one day produce up to 20 percent of the world's diamond supply. Human rights groups charge that the country's military seized control of the mine in late 2008, beating and raping civilians to force them from the area. Yet South Africa's government quickly agreed to buy Zimbabwe's uncut diamonds "outside" the Kimberley Process. Representatives of India's diamond industry, which buys uncut stones from around the world and produces about 95 percent of the world's finished diamonds, then upped pressure on their government to buy Mugabe's diamonds, helping to finance one of the world's most brutal dictatorships.[22]

Days later, a Kimberley Process summit meeting chaired by the Democratic Republic of Congo gave Mugabe the formal go-ahead to sell Marange stones "with immediate effect without supervision." Better to say yes than to say no and reveal the organization's impotence when members buy Mugabe's diamonds anyway. British and EU officials protested the decision, and the U.S.-based diamond group Rapaport quickly announced it wouldn't buy or sell Marange stones. But while Western mining companies and diamond-trading firms face an avalanche of bad press at home if they're caught cheating on these rules, that's not the case in many emerging-market states, where government and industry often exercise much greater direct influence over local media and where the demands of development often encourage governments to make and enforce their own rules.[23]

* * *

Finally, investors and companies can become G-Zero winners by recognizing these likely winners and losers—and placing their bets accordingly. Every stock picker looks great in a bull market, and that proved true in a world in which globalization lifted so many boats. The G-Zero will force investors to do a lot more homework. Those who do that work have much to gain.

LOSERS

The G-Zero is a process of creative destruction, as natural as it is inevitable. Institutions that no longer reflect the world they were created to promote and protect must give way to new ones. Those that struggle against this process of death and renewal are wasting time and resources that could be better spent on anticipating and shaping the post-G-Zero world. If leading established and emerging powers can't agree on a fair way to address global warming, boost global trade, manage food and public health crises, or govern cyberspace, they're unlikely to agree on how to divide decision-making power within new international institutions or on what to do with the old ones.

No, Western powers aren't doomed to permanent decline, but the most obvious near-term losers in the G-Zero era will be those who refuse to recognize the new reality and the need for change. Some U.S. and European policymakers will try to hang on for as long as possible to the institutions, rules, and standards that they created—which have traditionally protected their privileges—instead of working to shape the new institutions, rules, and standards that must eventually arise.

Referees

Perhaps the most obvious loser in a G-Zero world is a group we might call the *referees,* the institutions built to serve those who once dominated the international system but that can't be reformed quickly enough to remain effective. Take the North Atlantic Treaty Organization, the military alliance established in the Cold War's early days to provide collective defense against a Soviet advance into Western Europe. Hastings Lionel Ismay, the alliance's first secretary-general, famously said that NATO's true purpose was "to keep the Russians out, the Americans in, and the Germans down." But with the collapse of European and Soviet communism, we're now living in a world in which the Russians no longer threaten the West, America is less crucial for European security, and the Germans have emerged as Europe's most influential state. Still, a generation later, its mission accomplished, NATO muddles on.

Can the alliance serve a new purpose? In June 2011, in one of his final speeches as U.S. defense secretary, Robert Gates provided a startlingly frank appraisal of today's NATO, the sort of message that only someone preparing to exit the public stage could deliver. Gates recognized the rise of a new generation of European leaders and citizens for whom the Cold War was not a formative experience, but he then criticized those "willing and eager for American taxpayers to assume the growing security burden left by reductions in European defense budgets."[24] He warned that Washington could not continue to lead the alliance unless European governments contribute more money and more combat troops. Gates used the example of then-ongoing operations against Muammar Gadhafi's Libyan government to highlight the absurdity behind the problem: "The mightiest military alliance in history is only 11 weeks into an operation against a poorly armed regime in a sparsely populated country, yet many allies are beginning to run short of munitions, requiring the U.S., once more, to make up the difference."[25]

This was no routine complaint. It was a highly unusual warning that noted a fundamental fact of G-Zero life: The United States can no longer do more so that others can do less. For Washington to spend billions of dollars to lead so many reluctant followers and to sustain the life of an enormous institution that has not adapted to meet new challenges simply makes no sense. Perhaps alliance members can agree on a new mandate—and a new division of labor, burdens, and risks—but large institutions that have outlived their original purpose tend to lurch forward with no sense of direction until a crisis forces the creation of something new.

Though they will continue to do more than NATO to advance Western interests, organizations like the International Monetary Fund and World Bank will also be relative G-Zero losers. Africa is far from the only region where the China Development Bank and the Export-Import Bank of China are undermining the role these institutions play as international lenders of last resort—and their power to promote Western-backed political and economic reform inside developing countries. As noted earlier, in 2009 and 2010 China lent more money globally than the World Bank.[26] Not only are Chinese and other emerging-market lenders competing successfully against the IMF and the World Bank, but their governments continue to increase their influence within them. That trend, in turn, will undermine the effectiveness of these institutions as new voices debate their proper purpose from the inside.

In addition, many NGOs that monitor emerging states' compliance with Western standards of civil and human rights will be losers, as their principal supporters—established powers and increasingly anachronistic international institutions—lose their force. Authoritarian governments know that established powers no longer have the political and economic leverage to do much more than complain when aid groups and independent watchdogs are obstructed and harassed—or even ejected from these countries. Recent cases include the March 2011 shutdown of Human Rights Watch by the government of Uzbekistan and the ejection of the relief organization Doctors Without Borders from Bahrain in August 2011 during a crackdown on political protests there. Expect the number of examples to multiply in coming years.

Exposed States

The G-Zero will also heighten costs and risks for *exposed states*, those most deeply dependent on U.S. strength and Washington's willingness to use it to protect its allies. Centuries-old tensions between Japan and China are unlikely to ease anytime soon, because opportunistic officials on both sides too often score political points by feeding popular suspicion of the other—and because the wild-fire expansion of personal communications tools stokes national anger at unprecedented speed. Yet Japan's leaders know that China's regional clout will continue to expand, and they don't know how willing and able the United States will be to defend Japan's interests in years to come. Taiwan shares the same concerns.

Israel also falls squarely into this category. The 2011 uprisings in North Africa and the Middle East have given Arab citizens a new voice. Embattled leaders, both surviving autocrats and newly elected politicians, will have plenty of incentives to build street-level credibility by diverting attention from their own failings toward Israel's treatment of Palestinians. This is nothing new, but the combination of a lower U.S. profile in the Middle East and heightened competition for the region's hearts and minds between Gulf monarchs and Iran's mullahs will leave Israel more isolated than ever. Washington is not about to completely abandon Japan or Israel, but the need for a more frugal U.S. foreign policy and changes in their respective neighborhoods have already provoked considerable soul-searching in both countries on the need to question old assumptions and to develop alternative (and potentially expensive) new security strategies.

Shadow States

The next relative losers are the *shadow states,* those that would love to have the freedom of pivot states but remain frozen in the shadow of a single power. Mexico falls into this category because, for better and for worse, its economy and its standard of living are linked tightly with the health of the giant across the border. Mexico's largest sources of foreign currency come from oil sales, tourism, and remittances from Mexicans working abroad. In all three cases, the vast majority of that currency comes from the United States, and there is no evidence that this situation will change anytime soon.* Shadow states are not like Cold War–era satellites, countries where the government was thoroughly dominated by an outside power. Mexico is an important and independent emerging-market state. Its domestic and foreign policy choices are determined by its political process, not by the demands of outsiders. But as with other shadow states, the speed of Mexico's development and its commercial opportunities are defined almost entirely by conditions inside another country, one with enough geopolitical muscle and a large enough consumer market to define what is economically possible for its neighbor.

Ukraine offers another prime example of a shadow state. Despite public demand in much of the country to build stronger political, economic, and cultural relations with Europe, the government of this former Soviet republic accepts the practical necessity of protecting its traditional ties with Russia. About 17 percent of Ukraine's 46 million people identify themselves as ethnic Russians, making it tough for any politician to win national office in Ukraine without some support from the Russian community.[27] More important, Russia supplies most of Ukraine's energy and has demonstrated a willingness to use natural gas supplies as a foreign policy weapon. In the dead of winter in 2009, Gazprom, Russia's natural gas monopoly, cut supplies to Ukraine to build leverage in a dispute over pricing, and perhaps to remind Ukrainians that they continue to depend on their big brother to the east. Moscow would like Kiev to join a customs union that now includes Russia, Kazakhstan, and Belarus—a personal priority for Vladimir Putin—and has promised natural gas deliveries at substantially lower prices to sweeten the deal.[28] Given the stakes for energy security, that's an offer

---

* Given the importance of drug trafficking for organized crime and the flow of drugs across the border, even Mexico's informal economy is heavily dependent on U.S. demand.

Ukraine must take seriously, because lower gas prices can help political officials avoid both the need to hit voters with new energy taxes and the public backlash that would follow.

Ukraine would like to escape Russia's gravitational pull and become a pivot state, preserving relations with Russia while building new ties with Europe. In fact, Kiev would like to sign a free trade agreement with the European Union, a deal that would create tremendous commercial opportunities for the country and might eventually help Ukraine join the EU. But Russia has threatened to throw up new trade barriers if Kiev signs a deal with Europe, and the EU will end trade talks with Ukraine if it joins Russia's customs union. Add to that tangled web a network of politically connected Ukrainian businessmen pushing for closer ties with Russia than with Europe because they believe they're better able to handle commercial competition from the East than from the West. In short, Ukraine remains a shadow state and won't become a pivot state anytime soon, because it doesn't have the strength and independence to improve its bargaining position with either side. To preserve tomorrow's options, President Viktor Yanukovych would have to avoid much closer ties with either Russia or Europe. For now, Ukraine lives in Russia's long shadow.

Rogues Without Friends

Despite sometimes intense pressure from the superpower ninety miles to the north, Fidel Castro (and brother Raúl) have held power in Cuba for more than half a century. How? El Presidente got by with a little help from his powerful friends. First, there was the Soviet superpower patron. After the Soviet collapse, alongside a brief flirtation with China, Castro turned to Hugo Chávez and oil-rich Venezuela.

Some of the world's rogues are not so lucky. Libya's Muammar

Gadhafi held power for decades, but when he finally faced a critical challenge from his own people—always the biggest worry for an autocratic government—Gadhafi discovered how hard it is to survive in a world where no one likes you. Despite diplomatic overtures at various times, and European demand for Libya's energy exports, Gadhafi never had real friends in the West. His support for terrorism was already clear with the bombing of Pan Am Flight 103 over Lockerbie, Scotland, in December 1988. The Saudis accused Libya's leader of trying to assassinate then–crown prince Abdullah in 2003.[29] Iran had no great love for him either because it considered him an obstacle to Islamic revolution in North Africa, and though China built ties with Gadhafi over the years, its state-owned oil companies proved just as happy to work with Libyan rebels when push came to shove.[30] A lack of friends left Gadhafi fatally exposed when the tide of events turned against him. In the G-Zero era, everyone will need at least one powerful ally. Or a really deep bunker.

Dinosaurs

Among the companies least likely to prosper in a G-Zero world are the *dinosaurs,* those that cannot or will not adapt to a new environment. This group includes firms that benefited from Western-established rules of engagement and are unprepared to create operations flexible enough to keep pace with the changes the G-Zero will bring. Some technology companies will fail to prepare for a world where standards and rules change much more quickly and intellectual property rights are often in dispute. Many types of firms will find themselves competing with a much wider range of potential commercial rivals. Governments will rely increasingly on state-backed companies to extend their geopolitical and economic power. Some multinational corporations will be unprepared to face state-backed competitors, and they will be slow to react when governments of both established and emerging powers use market access, currency policy, capital controls, and more subtle tools to shape the commercial landscape within their borders and across their regions. Despite the advantages provided by governments, not all state-owned companies are well designed for competition. Some of them will miss market signals, because they're weighed down by political bureaucracy or by the operational limits that sometimes come with government backing. As they become less competitive, they will lose state support to other government-backed firms.

Remember the multibillion-dollar Beijiang Power and Desalination Plant, a project created and financed by China's top state planning agency? Today, this company is a protector. But the water the plant produces sells for just half of what it costs to produce, and the State Development & Investment Corporation is taking heavy losses to keep the plant afloat. For the moment, China's deep-pocketed government worries more over water shortages than over financial losses. But what happens when this project is no longer state of the art? Advances in water desalination—elsewhere in China and in other countries—are inevitable and will almost certainly be more cost-effective. In the not too distant future, the Beijiang Power and Desalination Plant could move from protector to dinosaur, abandoned in place. Publicly or privately owned, those able to meet G-Zero challenges will survive. Some will thrive. Dinosaurs will face extinction.

WINNERS *AND* LOSERS

Some will be both winners and losers in the G-Zero era. As mentioned above, Vietnam looks for the moment like a perfect pivot state. Yet, like so many other Asian countries benefiting from China's overflow—by drawing foreign investment, for example, as Chinese workers demand higher wages and become relatively more expensive for foreign companies to hire—it is increasingly falling under China's shadow. In the near term, these countries are winners, as they enjoy the runoff from the regional heavyweight's success. But over time, they can lose the ability to pivot and become trapped in the larger country's orbit. Remember: Winners have good options. Losers don't.

Today, Russia faces less outside pressure than at any moment since the outbreak of World War I. Its government has economic, geostrategic, and domestic policy reasons to try to reestablish its influence across former Soviet territory. (Putin's heavy-handed bid to draw Ukraine into that customs union with Kazakhstan and Belarus underlines the point.) In the early days of the G-Zero, Western governments will have fewer opportunities to interfere in that process. The EU is too busy refinancing some of its so-called peripheral states to want to entice new members looking to escape Russia's shadow, and many European countries continue to depend on Russia for a big portion of their energy supplies. Just as the Bush administration could do virtually nothing to intervene in Russia's war on Georgia in August 2008, Washington will exert less influence over time within Russia's sphere of influence.

That's the upside of G-Zero for Russia. The downside is that, as time passes, the Russian government and its companies will find themselves competing with China for influence and commercial contracts across Central Asia, and the growing self-confidence of pivot states like Turkey and Kazakhstan will limit Russia's room for maneuver. At home, global oil prices and their impact on Russia's financial health will play the largest role in determining whether the country remains politically stable. Lower prices could undermine confidence in the domestic economy, dividing Russia's leadership into warring factions. Higher oil prices would reinforce the control of the current elite and make it easier for policymakers to drag their feet on plans to diversify away from heavy reliance on the export of oil and gas. Either way, a near-term winner will become a longer-term loser.

Then there is the United States. The architects of U.S. foreign policy will have to do more with less in a G-Zero world, America will have fewer opportunities to get what it wants from other countries, and it's entirely likely that Americans will struggle to accept their diminished international role. That does not mean that the United States is destined to be a G-Zero loser. Resilience in the new era will depend on adaptability and the power to profit from the processes of creative destruction. This is a crucial American advantage. Throughout its history, the United States has valued innovation more than security, technological change more than traditional ways of doing things, and hope for the future more than veneration of the past. In a world of constant change, these qualities are likely to serve the country well. We will take a closer look at America's G-Zero future in the final chapter.

What About China?

Just as the United States is not set up to lose in the G-Zero world, China isn't necessarily well positioned to win. In the previous chapter, we looked at a few of the many opportunities that the G-Zero will provide China's government to reshape international politics and the global economy. Its position at the center of the fastest-growing region in the world offers opportunities to continue to welcome foreign investment in many economic sectors and to build enormously profitable trade ties in every direction. Its ability to extend its influence through and around existing international institutions, to use the country's vast market potential as a strategic resource, and to create and impose new technical rules and standards on the global business environment will only grow. For the next several years at least, the attraction of China's markets and its money will help the leadership brush aside criticism of its authoritarian politics.

But over the longer term, China has far too many internal challenges to take full advantage of the G-Zero environment. In 2007, Premier Wen Jiabao described China's economy as "unstable, unbalanced, uncoordinated, and ultimately unsustainable."[31] Those words have since been enshrined in the leadership's latest five-year plan, the blueprint for the next stage of China's rise. The country's primary problem is that it still depends too heavily for growth and the creation of new jobs on the spending habits of American, European, and Japanese consumers, a vulnerability never more obvious than in the immediate aftermath of the financial crisis, when the market meltdown inside China's best customers sent Beijing scrambling for ways to keep tens of millions of Chinese workers in their jobs. The leadership then launched state-driven job-creating projects to build out the country's infrastructure. The plan worked, but given how much China has already spent on these kinds of projects in recent years, pouring billions more into new roads, bridges, ports, and railways will eventually begin to yield diminishing returns.

In the fall of 2012, a new generation of Communist Party leaders will take center stage, and in 2013 China will have a new premier and a new government. The toughest and most important task these officials will face in a less predictable and more volatile G-Zero world is to overcome the party's deep risk aversion and resistance to change and to shift China's growth model from one that depends too heavily on exports to one that relies much more on Chinese people buying Chinese products. To accomplish that, the new party leadership will try to transfer huge amounts of wealth from the country's powerful state-owned companies to hundreds of millions of Chinese households. That's an enormous undertaking, particularly when so many power brokers within the governing elite have gotten rich off the old way of doing things. What's more, the scale and complexity of this project ensures that empowering Chinese consumers will be the work of a generation, not of a single five-year plan.

In the meantime, to increase its control over market conditions, Beijing will probably double down on state-run companies and state-directed lending. Though China's private sector continues to grow its share of the domestic economy, thirty-nine of the forty-two Chinese companies listed in the 2010 edition of the Fortune 500 were state-owned enterprises. Three-quarters of China's hundred largest publicly traded companies are government controlled.[32] Party officials with a stake in the success of these companies have amassed considerable power within the leadership and will use it to protect their privileges, like low-cost access to financing and land.

For now, Beijing will also have to accept that a bad day for America and Europe is still a bad day for China—and that G-Zero-related market turmoil will ensure that market volatility in all three places will become much more common. And it will have to face up to another hard reality: that the frictions created across Asia and around the world by China's rise are certain to generate new challenges that must be managed carefully. For a country that's already the world's number two economy and thought to be on its way to number one, things will become much more complicated in a region with so much G-Zero competition and so many hot spots.

Western bankers and economists have produced a range of forecasts in recent years on when China's economy will surpass America's, but every calculation is based on an assumption that China and the international environment in which it operates will undergo no game-changing transitions. That's what makes these forecasts so problematic in a G-Zero world. China must manage far too much internal change to make projections of its economic trajectory credible. After all, despite its economic miracle—in many ways, because of it—China numbers its annual supply of large-scale protests in the tens of thousands. For 2006, its Academy of Social Sciences reported 60,000 "mass group incidents," an official euphemism for demonstrations of public anger that involve at least fifty people. In 2007, the reported number reached 80,000. A leak of no-longer-published official figures put the number for 2008 at 127,000, and estimates reached 180,000 by 2010.[33] No reliable more recent data are available, but there is no reason to believe that the tensions that produced these eruptions have eased.

A traffic accident in Henan province sends police scrambling to contain more than a thousand rioters. A chemical spill into a Chinese river cuts water supplies to Harbin, a city of four million people, sparking public fury. In Hunan, a farmer pushed off his land by property developers sets himself on fire, provoking protests that spread quickly from town to town. In Inner Mongolia, a Han Chinese truck driver kills a local herdsman in a hit-and-run accident, and ethnic unrest flares for days. Rioting in Xinjiang province spins out of control, forcing a state Internet shutdown across an area three times the size of California. In a Chinese coastal city, security guards sent to break up a protest by migrant workers push a pregnant woman to the ground. The news hits the Internet, igniting a firestorm that only paramilitary forces in armored personnel carriers can handle. Thousands of people assault government buildings and set police cars ablaze.

China is not on the verge of chaos. Its security forces are the world's best at containing large-scale riots, and these protests are not yet coordinated by any form of coherent opposition to Communist Party control. Nor is the Internet China's ticking time bomb. The consulting firm McKinsey & Company forecasts that there will be 750 million Chinese online by 2015, and security officials can't follow every email and text message, but they can still monitor China's blogosphere, where unfiltered ideas find their largest potential audience.[34] Most demonstrations are still directed at local officials and are fueled by local grievances. Three decades of double-digit growth and rising economic expectations in China's cities have earned the leadership reserves of public patience. Unlike the Middle East, where sectarian, ethnic, and tribal divisions can divide loyalties within the armed forces, the Han Chinese–dominated People's Liberation Army and security police will not side with ethnic minorities against the regime. All these factors reinforce continued domestic stability. But if these simmering tensions are unlikely to ignite a revolution, they can't help but impact China's economic trajectory. Profound changes are sweeping across the country, and their potential effect on China's growth could be severe if a future slowdown puts too many workers on the streets at once.

China's demographics will provide another serious test. Its population is getting older, as the one-child policy and other factors leave fewer young people to support retirees. By 2030, nearly 180 million Chinese will have passed the age of sixty, and the need to expand and reinforce a formal social safety net to provide pensions and health care for hundreds of millions of uninsured people will add unprecedented costs. Aware of the problem, many young adults are saving their money, both to support their parents and eventually to protect their own retirement. That trend will make the state's drive to increase household spending far more difficult to achieve and will ensure that young couples are more likely to produce just one child, exacerbating the demographic challenge.

In addition, given that so much of China's growth is still coming from infrastructure projects and other state-directed investments, the impact on an already overtaxed environment could shock the system. Land degradation, lowered air quality, and water shortages are urgent and growing issues. The country's capacity to tolerate a deteriorating environment is higher than in most developing markets—to say nothing of the developed world—but the chances for an environmental incident to provoke a dangerously destabilizing event are growing. The water question alone will keep policymakers busy for years. As rising prices and demands for higher wages undermine low-end manufacturing capacity, China's economy may not make the leap to the next stage of its maturity. Increased state spending on research and development will help, but without a social, educational, and political system that encourages innovation, entrepreneurship, and independent thinking, change will come slowly. That's why most of the progress on emerging technologies—biogenetics, nanotechnology, and even alternative energy—are unlikely to come from China.

Even if China's leadership makes major unexpected progress on domestic reform, it will find that the international environment is becoming less friendly to its expansion. Higher prices for the oil, gas, metals, and minerals China needs to power its economy will weigh on growth. The development of all those other emerging-market players will only add to the upward pressure on food and other commodity prices, undermining public confidence in government, the most important source of China's baseline social stability. In addition, as state-backed Chinese companies draw their government into the political and economic lives of so many other countries, particularly in the developing world, they will risk the same backlash from local companies and workers that plagues so many other foreign firms doing business far from home. And because the Chinese government has such a direct stake in the success of these companies, Beijing will be drawn into conflicts it has never coped with before, with leadership that might not agree on how best to respond to any sudden convulsion of organized protest, exactly what happened in the lead-up to the Tiananmen Square crackdown—and at a time before modern tools of communication made it much easier for protesters to coordinate plans.

That's why, in a G-Zero world, China is the major power least likely to develop along a predictable path. India, Brazil, and Turkey can continue to grow for the next ten years with the same basic formula that triggered their growth over the past ten. The United States, Europe, and Japan will reinvest in economic systems that have a long history of success. China must undertake enormously complex and ambitious reforms to continue its drive to become a modern, middle-class power. The country's rise is unstable, unbalanced, uncoordinated, and unsustainable—and the Communist Party leadership knows that its ability to guide China through the next stage of its development is far from certain.

* * *

Today, the G20 and other international institutions produce positive results only when a working majority of the world's most powerful states are threatened with the same problem at the same moment. In the not too distant future, America, Europe, and China will all need an international system that reinforces their collective stability. By then, the G-Zero will have inflicted enough damage on each of them to create demand for something new.

What might that something new look like? That's a question for the next chapter.

CHAPTER FIVE

What Comes Next?

If you are going through hell, keep going.
—Winston Churchill

The G-Zero is not the new normal, because it cannot be sustained. But just as it took World War II to lift the United States to superpower status and beget the Bretton Woods system, so it will probably take another calamity, or at least the credible threat that one is imminent, to give birth to a new international order. Aristotle argued that matter will always move to fill a vacuum, and in international politics self-interest will finally force those with the means to bring about change to accept the costs, sacrifices, and risks needed to fill the G-Zero power vacuum with something else.

Governments don't accept costs and risks until they believe they have to—and until they become convinced that other governments won't do it for them. But to protect their domestic political positions, leaders of established powers will act to try to ensure that transnational challenges don't threaten their countries' security, wealth, and privileges. Political elites in emerging states will try to make certain that crises don't prevent their countries from emerging. As the G-Zero generates turmoil, decision makers in both sets of countries will have to build new systems, alliances, and global institutions. They will work together or act separately. They will adapt existing international institutions or build new ones. Either way, the G-Zero is not the new world order. It's a period of transition that will give way to something else.

We cannot know whether the G-Zero will last five years or fifteen, but we know that while it exists, it is an incubator of catastrophe. Nor can we know what this catastrophe might look like. A meltdown in European financial markets sparks a banking crisis much larger than the 2008 version, and this time feuding political officials don't move quickly enough to contain the fallout. Or an influenza epidemic in Asia goes global because leaders of hot-zone countries rely on secrecy to cover their backs rather than the transparency needed to build an effective international response. Or North Korea implodes, setting off a flow of refugees across borders, putting hostile neighbors on high alert, provoking disputes over who will pay to rebuild, and triggering a race to lock down the country's nuclear material. Or a spectacular terrorist attack in India triggers a war with nuclear-armed Pakistan. Or warming-related changes in weather patterns create severe droughts in some places and floods in others, unleashing a food crisis that brings down multiple governments in the Middle East, Asia, and Africa. Or some combination of these problems sends energy costs surging and the economies of the world's leading energy importers into turmoil.

But this chapter is not about the crises that might compel collective action. It's about what comes next and who will lead. To predict what the new international order will look like, we must answer two questions in particular. First, will the United States and China act as partners or enemies? No political and commercial relationship is more important for twenty-first-century peace and prosperity. Second, will other countries have the strength to play an important, independent role in the international order?

Some of the problems and opportunities that will shape the future of U.S.-Chinese relations depend on developments inside each country. Confrontation becomes more likely if one or both of them suffer serious economic setbacks that send leaders scrambling for foreign scapegoats. In China, policymakers face the profoundly complicated task of implementing the reforms needed to keep the country's economy humming while managing the threats that all these changes pose to the country's domestic tranquility. In Washington, if partisan rivalries continue to poison American politics and prevent lawmakers from restoring the country to fiscal health, U.S. frustration with the U.S.-Chinese trade imbalance could reach a boiling point. In 2012, the transition to the next generation of Chinese leaders begins with a new president and a new Politburo in Beijing. In November, U.S. voters go to the polls for both presidential and congressional elections. For better or for worse, all these new legislators and decision makers will change the relationship.

Then there are the factors determined by direct interaction between the two countries. If U.S. companies continue to earn large profits inside China, they will have a stake in China's success and in stable U.S.-Chinese relations. That would give them good reasons

to lobby the White House and U.S. lawmakers to avoid unneces-
sary confrontations. If, on the other hand, Chinese companies use
their growing leverage within China's bureaucracy to craft new
rules and regulations that tip the competitive playing field in their
direction, U.S. companies are likely to drive the two governments
toward a more aggressive commercial competition. If China continues to allow its currency to appreciate against the dollar, we could
see a healthy rebalancing of U.S.-Chinese trade relations—and less
demand in Washington for punitive legislative action. But a major
cyberattack launched by someone on one side against someone on
the other—or even the appearance of one—might spark a politically reckless response. A shock that sends oil prices sharply higher
will give U.S. and Chinese officials a powerful common interest in
easing the resulting pain, but a coup in North Korea, depending on
how it develops, or a fight over Iran, would likely put U.S. and
Chinese officials on opposite sides of a security crisis.

A G1 scenario in which the United States dominates the global
order with anything like the international leverage it had following
World War II is extremely unlikely. That would imply the kind of
internal turmoil in China that would be felt in the United States.
Volatility in China will create headaches on Wall Street—and,
given the importance of Chinese demand for global growth, a collapse of China's economy would be the shot heard round the world.
In fact, given the connections in their economies and the interde-
pendencies that remain in the global economy, it would also be hard
for America to be strong if Europe is weak. The combination of
circumstances needed for a return to 1945 is more than today's U.S.
economy could handle. That brings us to the second question most
likely to determine the shape of the post-G-Zero world: the pro-
jected strength of other powerful states. Will global leadership be
more broadly divided among several established and emerging

states? Can pivot states continue to pivot, or do many of them begin to behave more like satellites?

If the European Union's core and peripheral economies can harmonize policies and reestablish stability in the Eurozone, Europe will remain a force to be reckoned with. If Japan can reinvigorate economic growth and develop a political system that enjoys long-term public confidence, it can again become an important global power. If India can further liberalize its economy, avoid a food price shock, and manage the coming acceleration in the flow of migrants from the countryside into its cities, it can become a much more significant international player. If Turkey can avoid a crippling internal showdown that pits the ruling party and its emphasis on reform of laws on religious expression against secularists within the business, media, and military elite, and if economic reform remains at the top of the agenda, its government can continue to expand the country's role as a formidable power broker. In the not too distant future, power in Saudi Arabia will pass from the current generation of leaders to the next. If the new royals can reform their way toward a political system that can be sustained over the longer term, or if rising oil revenues and increased state spending can keep pressure for reform at bay, the Saudis can then use their leadership of the Gulf Cooperation Council to extend their dominance across the region. If Brazil's government can keep inflation in check, further reduce the gap between rich and poor, and wisely manage development of the country's natural wealth, Brazil will entrench its position as Latin America's most influential state.

By placing U.S.-Chinese relations along one axis of a graph and the relative strength of other countries along the other, we can map the four likeliest post-G-Zero scenarios (see page 156).

The grid gives us four distinct alternatives. If the crises triggered by the G-Zero push the United States and China closer

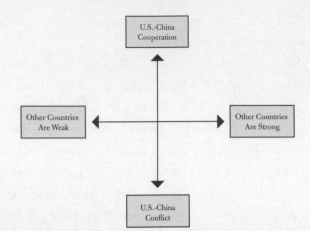

together, and if these two are by far the world's most powerful states, then we are likely to see the emergence of an international system in which Washington and Beijing find benefit in burden sharing. We can call this scenario the *G2*. But if a generally cooperative United States and China share leadership with other strong states, we might see a kind of *concert* of nations and real cooperation within a G20-like institution.

If the United States and China emerge much stronger than any conceivable coalition of other states, and if the G-Zero pushes them toward a much more hostile relationship, we're likely to see the development of *Cold War 2.0*. In this system, rivalry between great powers forces others to choose sides or to struggle to remain outside either orbit. But if Washington and Beijing find themselves at odds in a world with several other strong states, global power will fragment, and we will see a *world of regions* in international decision making. These scenarios represent extremes, of course, and the future will probably provide some combination of at least two of these scenarios.

That said, the basic options break down as shown on page 157. The pages that follow detail each of these four broad scenarios.

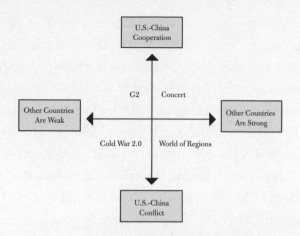

THE G2—A U.S.-CHINESE PARTNERSHIP

Over the past decade, two wars and mounting debt have spurred calls by some Americans for Washington to share the burdens of leadership, and China has emerged as a potential partner. In September 2005, then–U.S. deputy secretary of state Robert Zoellick used a speech to the National Committee on U.S.-China Relations to call on Beijing to act as a "responsible stakeholder" in international politics. China's growth had given the country a stake in global peace and stability, and Washington welcomed any bid by Beijing to invest more deeply in the American-designed international system. Zoellick has continued to argue that the United States welcomes China's peaceful rise and that the two countries can work together to forge solutions for the world's most intractable problems.

American economist C. Fred Bergsten was the first to popularize the term "G2" to symbolize a U.S.-Chinese strategic partnership that could bring about much-needed change in international politics. In his 2005 book *The United States and the World Economy,* he argued that none of the world's most pressing challenges could be effectively addressed without cooperation between Washington and Beijing. Bergsten insists that a G2 doesn't undermine the importance of institutions that represent the needs and aspirations of other countries or that act as lenders of last resort.[1] But the United States and China are the leading established and emerging markets, respectively. They are the world's two largest economies and two largest trading nations. China is the world's largest creditor state, and the United States has become the world's largest debtor state. America and China are the world's two largest polluters. There is no way to rebalance the world economy, breathe life into global trade talks, take on climate change, and manage other transnational problems without coordinated leadership and burden sharing from America and China.

Historian Niall Ferguson and economist Moritz Schularick coined the term "Chimerica" to describe the seemingly symbiotic economic relationship that had formed between the two countries, lifting the entire global economy.[2] They suggested that U.S.-Chinese mutual dependence had created a single economic engine, one that extended across 13 percent of the earth's surface and represented a quarter of its population, a third of its economic output, and 40 percent of its growth between 1998 and 2007.*

A U.S.-Chinese partnership need not be institutionalized. Former U.S. national security advisor Zbigniew Brzezinski has proposed an "informal G2," a "comprehensive partnership" grounded in the two countries' complex interdependence that would provide coordinated leadership on security issues from the nuclear programs in Iran and North Korea to relations between Indians and Pakistanis and Israelis and Palestinians. Brzezinski describes his vision of G2 as a "mission worthy of the two coun-

---

* They warned, however, that debt was the tie that bound the two together and later argued that the financial crisis had killed what had always been an unnatural alliance.

tries with the most extraordinary potential for shaping our collective future."[3]

China's leaders have made clear that their country isn't yet ready for such a demanding role and won't be anytime soon.[4] But if things change in the years to come, what would it take for Washington and Beijing to form this kind of post-G-Zero partnership? First, Beijing would have to decide that China can afford to behave as a developed state. That's not simply a matter of becoming the world's largest economy. China's leaders and its people would have to see cooperation with Washington as a cost-effective way to reinforce a global system that is working to China's advantage. It means building a broad, prosperous, and self-confident middle class that can become a much more formidable force in Chinese politics. China must become a true stakeholder, not because someone in Washington pushes the idea, but because a critical mass of senior Chinese officials comes to believe that a G2 serves China's national interests. This is not a case of China working its way toward America; it's a meeting of mutual interest.

In addition, only if China develops a commercial elite that values the rule of law and protection of intellectual property rights—for Chinese and foreign citizens, companies, and investors—can the country's governing institutions earn a local legitimacy that extends beyond party control of police and soldiers. Here again, this change must take place not as a response to demands from outsiders, but because Chinese officials accept that it serves China's long-term strength. Legitimacy at home is essential for leadership abroad.

China will also have to create sustainable balance in its economy, by shifting its reliance for growth from its current heavy dependence on exports toward greater consumption at home—but without "decoupling" from Western consumers to a degree that would isolate China from the world's other largest economies. Further, over time many of the country's largest state-owned enterprises will outlive their usefulness. As with other dying institutions, those who profit from them will fight to keep them alive, and state officials will be tempted to artificially extend their life spans. Creative destruction can be either a powerful source of prosperity or a frightening source of turmoil, but only by letting these enterprises die a natural death and enabling more dynamic companies to take their place can China continue to extend its economic gains. That is the lesson of adapters and dinosaurs, and it ultimately applies to China just as surely as to America and Europe.

While China will extend its military power in years to come, particularly in East and South Asia, a G2 depends for the foreseeable future on Beijing's willingness to rely on American military might to provide most global public goods outside of Asia. Arms races and fights over spheres of influence can sometimes take on a dangerous life of their own, and Beijing's ability to rebalance its economy and to create a solid social safety net for an aging population will require that Chinese policymakers spend no more than necessary on an extension of the country's hard power.

The second requirement for emergence of a G2 order is that the U.S. economy recover enough of its vitality to persuade American taxpayers they can afford to invest again in a more expansive foreign policy. U.S. lawmakers will have to move beyond the current partisan paralysis toward a political culture that does not breed U.S. public and political hostility toward Beijing.

A G2 is also more likely to develop if the G-Zero generates the kind of crisis that aligns U.S. and Chinese interests. If economic or political factors send crude oil prices soaring, the world's two largest energy consumers will have a clear and compelling interest in working together either to solve the problem that pushed prices higher or to cooperate on development of hydrocarbon alternatives.

If both countries face successful large-scale cyberattacks, by anarchists or any other group without ties to either side, U.S. and Chinese officials might work together to establish a common defense. Open conflict between India and Pakistan could also lead Washington and Beijing to jointly broker a deal to prevent a nuclear exchange. If North Korea were to collapse, the two governments might have an interest, depending on how events unfold, in ensuring that the country's nuclear weapons remain secure. Combine enough of these challenges, and partnership on security issues might become a habit.

Finally, a G2 world is one in which no other power or alliance of powers has the political and economic muscle to compete with America or China. In this scenario, European powers fail to harmonize policies and the union is divided from within or muddles through to a less dynamic future. Japan's political dysfunction continues, and its government is unable to fully reinvigorate its economy. Following an international market meltdown or for reasons particular to each country, emerging powers like India, Brazil, and Turkey simply fail to emerge fully enough to cement a strong independent role for themselves even within their respective regions. This is a world in which U.S. and Chinese leadership would be indispensable.

Many of the arguments that some consider obstacles to U.S.-Chinese cooperation are unlikely to pose serious long-term roadblocks. For example, officials in Washington (and several other capitals) have criticized China's currency policy. They charge that by holding the value of the yuan at artificially low levels relative to the dollar (and other currencies), China is maintaining an unfair trade advantage. But between July 2005 and July 2011, the yuan rose by nearly 30 percent against the dollar.[5] As Beijing works to reduce China's dependence on exports and to shift wealth toward Chinese consumers, officials will likely continue to allow the yuan to edge its way north—not because outsiders demand it, but because the Chinese leadership believes it serves Chinese interests. This is not an issue that will prevent the U.S. and Chinese governments from working together when both sides think it necessary.

Recent years have brought a significant jump in the number of U.S. and Chinese officials lobbing insults at one another across the Pacific. That's in large part a result of the ongoing political transitions in each country. For a particularly colorful example of this trend, look for a YouTube video called "Chinese Professor,"[6] an expensively made television commercial produced by a U.S. interest group called Citizens Against Government Waste. Set in "2030 AD," the ad features a Chinese lecturer in a large, high-tech auditorium speaking to university-age Chinese students about failed empires of the past. The clip ends with the professor noting that "now [the Americans] work for us!" as the students share a collective laugh at America's foolishness. In "Fight the Debt Limit Extension"—an even less subtle ad from Mark Amodei, a Republican candidate for Congress from Nevada—a Chinese broadcaster explains (in dubbed English with Mandarin subtitles) how President Barack Obama made the United States subservient to China. Following a quick clip of Obama bowing to Chinese president Hu Jintao, a wave of Chinese troops marches triumphantly through Washington.[7] Amodei won his race by a wide margin.

Though China's media and lower-level state officials sometimes feed these bursts of politically inspired paranoia with provocative public comments, such ads are aimed not at Chinese autocrats but at American democrats. This is election-year politics. Some politicians in the United States want to prove their toughness by taking on China—or prove their ideological orthodoxy by tarring the other party with collaboration with China's Communist Party.

This isn't new. In 1989, Democrats seized on photographs of National Security Advisor Brent Scowcroft toasting Chinese officials during a secret diplomatic visit to Beijing just six months after the massacre in Tiananmen Square.[8] During the 1992 presidential campaign, candidate Bill Clinton scolded President George H. W. Bush for engaging the "butchers of Beijing," but that didn't stop Clinton once president from offering China permanent normalized trade relations.[9] Nor did it stop China's leaders from accepting his outstretched hand.

By the same token, Chinese officials entered the power transition process in their country in 2012 looking to burnish their reputation for toughness for the benefit of China's hard-liners. But their public posturing won't slow the flow of U.S. companies entering China in search of long-term profits. Nor will it discourage influential Chinese public officials from profiting from U.S. and other foreign investment or prevent Chinese exporters from pushing their government to maintain strong enough ties with Washington to keep U.S. markets open.

Still, a G2 remains unlikely to develop. First, as noted, China wants no part of a G2 today and might feel no more confident about the country's ability to play this role in the future. In recent years, Beijing's response to calls for greater international burden sharing has included two distinct warnings. Despite more than three decades of go-go growth, they have insisted, China remains a developing state—with all the special needs and vulnerabilities that come with that status. The next complicated, dangerous stages of China's development, they warn, will leave the country's leaders with too many domestic long-term challenges to accept new global responsibilities. They also have let it be known that China does not welcome attempts by Washington to define Beijing's "responsibilities" in international politics. Many people have called for a G2 in recent years, but none of them are Chinese. The volatile G-Zero era is unlikely to change that.

Further, it's hard to find historical precedent for any durable multidimensional partnership between the world's two most powerful states, particularly when they have such different political and economic systems. Unless events lead China toward fundamental political reform and away from state dominance of markets, no G-Zero-related trend or event will align their interests for very long. And if those reforms fail, China's people will find someone to blame. Whether that someone lives in Beijing or abroad, a G2 becomes that much more difficult to sustain.

In addition, the G2 scenario would demand that both America and China emerge from the G-Zero with a new self-confidence. That's especially unlikely given how ambitious China's economic reform plans are and how difficult it will be for an increasingly insecure American middle class to accept a rebalancing of the two economies that leaves it with much less purchasing power than before. A newly self-confident Chinese middle class might not want to see its government work more closely with Washington. Just as likely, national rivalries will become more intense, and Chinese officials will use public suspicion of Washington to enhance Beijing's international bargaining position or to build its popularity with expressions of patriotic defiance.

In fact, given the frustration and fear that rebalancing will arouse in both countries, China might well find more in common with a country like Germany than with the United States. Like China, Germany is a lender, not a borrower. Its trade balance is second only to China's among the world's leading economies. As China looks to hedge its bets on the dollar, for example, Beijing and Berlin will develop a common interest in bolstering the strength of the euro—and of European institutions more generally. Germany will not become a superpower for the foreseeable future. Its economy and population are a small fraction of America's or China's, and becoming a military power once again would require a huge shift in Germany's political culture, considerable time, and hundreds of billions of euros. The limited international use of its language would also undermine any bid to expand Germany's cultural influence. But its economic and diplomatic leverage, particularly within Europe, is considerable. This is potentially one of the world's most important pivot states. With Europe's most powerful and resilient economy, Germany might find enough common ground with China during a period of global rebalancing to sharply limit the need for China to partner with America.

Nor are G-Zero crises that push America and China closer together necessarily more likely than those that might drive them apart. A full implosion in North Korea is as likely to produce U.S.-Chinese conflict as cooperation. U.S. officials would probably insist on Korean reunification—though that would come with a price tag no single state can afford, far in excess of Germany's reunion, because today's South Korean economy is not as strong as West Germany's in 1990 and North Korea has nowhere near the resources that kept East Germany alive. Beijing, on the other hand, might well argue for a new North Korean government, one allied to China and with a Chinese-inspired commitment to gradual economic reform. That's the kind of disagreement that would push America closer to Japan, not China.

Nor is it clear that another Indian-Pakistani confrontation would impel Washington and Beijing to work more closely together. Depending on how the conflict began and how it developed, China might side with Pakistan to help contain a rising India, while the United States might support India to help limit China's Asian expansion, to establish potentially more lucrative trade ties, to boost relations with a fellow democracy, and to neutralize a threat of Islamic militancy inside Pakistan.

Further, it's hard to imagine that China and America will be the only two countries to emerge from the G-Zero with their ambitions intact. Whatever happens to the Eurozone, the German, French, and other governments have invested decades of political capital in the dream of Europe whole and free. Its highly educated workforce, its tradition of innovation, and the resilience of its institutions provide ample reason for confidence that Europe can overcome its current challenges. Japan has suffered many setbacks—but it is still the world's third largest economy in spite of them. Nor is there any reason to believe that growth in emerging states like India, Brazil, Turkey, and others will be stunted to an extent that robs them of their steadily increasing international influence. Their growth may slow, but only a truly global disaster will send them back to 1970.

CONCERT—A G20 THAT ACTUALLY WORKS

Can the G-Zero itself force broader international cooperation? Imagine a world in which Washington and Beijing alone cannot dominate, where it's unavoidably obvious that international problems can be solved only with the engagement of other powerful countries. This is a world like the one we already live in—with one crucial difference. In this scenario, a sense of emergency ensures that established and emerging powers work together, compromise, and share the risks and burdens of leadership. It's a G20 that *actually works*.

This scenario implies a kind of "concert of nations," an international structure similar to the so-called Concert of Europe that aligned Britain, the Russian Empire, Austria, Prussia, and eventually France in a nineteenth-century partnership designed to restore order and keep the peace in Europe following the upheaval of the French Revolution and the carnage of the Napoleonic Wars. By 1815, the continent's monarchs saw an opportunity to restore their former authority. The result was the institutionalization of a balance of power that created relative stability in Europe until the outbreak of World War I nearly a century later.*

As we've seen, today's G20, the closest thing we now have to a concert of nations, produces real results only when its most important members feel threatened by exactly the same crisis at exactly the same moment—and the threat has to be imminent. For the G-Zero era to produce a concert scenario, it must first create a series of crises—or one really big one—that force governments to cooperate. The financial crisis and the Copenhagen climate summit illustrate just how hard it will be to accomplish that. In the fall of 2008, established and emerging powers faced a banking and credit crisis that storm walls could not hold. All these countries knew that the floodwaters were dangerous, but none of them knew just how cold and deep the water really was. Fear produced real cooperation—the G20 framework for reform of global financial regulations, for example, and a process for rebalancing the IMF—but with each passing month it became clear that though everyone was taking on water, some were in a lot more trouble than others. Disagreements emerged over how to respond to the crisis. Americans argued for stimulus, Europeans insisted on austerity, and China looked to speed the process of reducing its long-term economic dependence on both. China, India, and Brazil emerged from the crisis much more quickly and easily than did the established powers.

---

* That said, this period featured several smaller wars and revolutions.

Each country felt it could afford to ignore calls for collective action and look to domestic challenges. At Copenhagen, each government understood that global warming was a global issue. But calculations of individual interests revealed that here, too, some would suffer much more than others. More to the point, the threat did not appear imminent. For emerging powers like China and India, the impact of sharp reductions in carbon emissions on economic growth and job creation were far less abstract than the impact of climate change coordination on the melting of the polar ice caps.

Many types of crisis might prove large enough effects to force institutional cooperation. Imagine a meltdown in European financial markets that goes much further than the 2008 version in the United States. Trouble in smaller economies then spills over into larger economies that are too big to bail. Germany and the other core European countries balk at leading a rescue effort. Recriminations fly, and banks in core countries with exposure to bad loans in other countries can't be saved. The Eurozone collapses, and Europe fragments. Both the United States and China lose a critical trade partner and the jobs that it supports. The impact is felt throughout the developing world. The problem here is that, as with the financial crisis of 2008, the effects of even a much greater shock to the system will last longer in some places than in others, and the temptation to find advantage in the weakness of others could easily prove too great to resist.

Or a food price shock takes hold. Rising global demand for grain outstrips supply, and a series of bolt-from-the-blue weather-related disasters sends food prices soaring across South and Southeast Asia, North Africa, much of Latin America, and parts of the former Soviet Union. Large-scale protests in Russia provoke a brutal state crackdown that strips the current government of most of its popularity. Uprisings in India can't be contained. Venezuela, Thailand, and Egypt descend into chaos. Violence escalates in China. But as noted earlier, food shocks will always hit emerging powers and the developing world much harder than the United States, Europe, and Japan because grain prices account for a smaller percentage of the price of food in these countries and because the people who live there spend most of their money on other things. This is not a crisis that can hit everyone at once.

In addition, food crises are as likely to lead to finger-pointing as to cooperation. In early 2011, an outbreak of *E. coli* in Germany prompted accusations from German officials that contaminated Spanish cucumbers were to blame. In response, Russia banned the import of all fresh vegetables from the European Union.[10] Spain's cucumbers were later shown to be completely blameless, and the country's agriculture minister demanded compensation for falsely accused farmers.[11] If a full-blown food scare or public health catastrophe occurred, the only coordination between countries might be their attempts to quarantine first and ask questions later. Finally, compounding the anger on both sides of the *E. coli* scare was the problem that it happened at the height of the fight over austerity, as German politicians warned that Germany's taxpayers would provide financial help for Spain's struggling government only if it enacted pay cuts, tax hikes, and other measures that limit state spending on pensions and health care.

Or a cyberattack of unknown origin takes down power grids in the United States, across Europe, and in China in quick succession. Various groups claim credit, but policymakers in both established and emerging countries are forced to accept that they don't know how the attacks happened, who carried them out, or why. Everyone suspects everyone else, and all feel a new vulnerability. But just as terrorist attacks can generate international empathy and create ad hoc coalitions in response, these alliances are not particularly durable. The United States, Europe, China, India, and Russia all face threats from Islamic militants. But even if an al Qaeda–like organization were to hit all these places at once, cooperation between these countries would probably be limited—and it wouldn't last long. Why would responses to cyberattacks be any different?

Ultimately, it's hard to imagine a crisis large enough to force lasting cooperation from most of the world's established and emerging powers. What's more, the complexity of the challenges facing the foreign ministers of nineteenth-century Europe pales beside those of the G-Zero era. A nineteenth-century European system that depended on the willingness of a handful of monarchs to work together doesn't translate well into a twenty-first-century global model made up of dozens of powerful countries with different sets of political and economic values and at different stages of development. World War II gave rise to Bretton Woods only because the United States was ready to lead. Without U.S. power, the new order would not have come to be. An earlier effort at global institution building had already fallen short for exactly this reason. World War I gave rise to the League of Nations, an organization that failed to prevent World War II mainly because the government that promised leadership, the United States, could not deliver. That's why a concert scenario is even less likely than a G2 model to come to pass.

COLD WAR 2.0—OR SOMETHING WORSE

Over the past decade, several commentators have warned that America and China are on one form or another of collision course. There's even a board game on the market called Red Dragon Rising: The Coming War with China. *Strategy & Tactics* magazine calls the game "a strategic-level investigation, with operational undertones, of the possibilities inherent in the first 30-or-so days of a hypothetical war between the People's Republic of China and a U.S.-led counter-alliance."[12]

Let's hope it doesn't come to that. But if China and the United States are headed for more direct forms of conflict, and if they have far more economic, political, and military power than any other country or bloc of countries in the post-G-Zero order, then we are more likely to see a scenario we might call Cold War 2.0. This is not a war likely to be waged with fighter jets launched from aircraft carriers. The new weapons of war will probably be economic: market access, investment rules, and currency values. We could also see a series of cyberattacks and counterstrikes designed to disrupt information flows or even to target the other side's critical infrastructure. We should not assume that we have any idea who would hold the advantage in such a face-off—or that those who might wage this war do either.

Cold War 2.0 could develop in several ways. Chinese policymakers come to believe that an increasingly cash-poor Washington no longer has the resources for a fight halfway around the world, and the Chinese military elite uses its leverage within the leadership to exert economic pressure intended to drive the United States from its Asian sphere of influence. Washington then decides that, given U.S. interests in the region, it can't afford not to push back. Or one side absorbs a destructive cyberattack on its military, its financial markets, or its electrical grid and becomes convinced, rightly or wrongly, that the other side has committed a premeditated act of war. Retaliation follows, and the conflict spirals. Or maybe a defective Chinese product kills dozens of U.S. consumers, igniting a trade war that takes on a life of its own. A seemingly endless number of such potential flash points could provoke many different forms of fighting, and this confrontation might force other states to take sides.

As to what any confrontation might look like, it's tempting to fall back on the Cold War model—two superpowers staring one another down from behind their nuclear arsenals with only the threat of mutually assured destruction stilling hands. But that scenario ignores an important point. During the U.S.-Soviet conflict, the Iron Curtain was not just the prison wall that kept invaders out and prisoners in. It was a buffer between the capitalist and communist worlds. The Soviet Union was an important energy supplier for Europe, but other East–West trade ties were extremely limited. The world was a more zero-sum place in which one side could inflict harm on the other without damaging its own interests. Today's U.S.-Chinese relations, on the other hand, will continue to rest on a degree of interdependence—a "mutually assured *economic* destruction"—that makes it difficult for the two sides to damage each other without damaging themselves. The United States needs China to continue to finance U.S. debt. China needs to be sure that Americans can and will pay them back—and that the currency they use will be worth more than the paper it's printed on. That's a stabilizing force in the relationship.

It's also important to keep this interdependence in mind when looking over the more traditional list of supposedly likely U.S.-Chinese flash points. In 2006, author Ted Galen Carpenter published *America's Coming War with China: A Collision Course over Taiwan,* in which he sketched a scenario in which a U.S.-Chinese conflict over Taiwan in 2013 provokes a quarter century of confrontation as "the world's two leading powers [become] locked in a Cold War . . . at least as intense as the earlier surly confrontation between the United States and the Soviet Union."[13]

Taiwan has enough friends in the U.S. Congress to ensure that U.S. arms sales to the island will continue, provoking the occasional diplomatic dustup. But China has long since co-opted much of Taiwan's business elite with offers of sweetheart commercial deals on the mainland and by signing an unprecedented trade agreement with the island in 2010.* In the process, Beijing has ensured that many of Taiwan's most influential voices sing the praises of steady cross-Strait relations. Only a Taiwanese declaration of independence could provoke an open conflict, and that won't happen because Taiwan knows that Washington won't support it, Taipei can't afford it, and most Taiwanese don't want it.

This scenario also depends on the relative weakness of the world's other states. The beginnings of an all-consuming U.S.-Chinese conflict could force other countries to take sides or try to hedge between the two. But it's much harder for a pivot state to play one side off another when the two sides are engaged in some form of direct conflict. A militarily aggressive China might drive Japan, South Korea, and even India toward much closer ties with the United States, and Washington could then afford to extend its presence in Asia by pooling its strength with these and other regional powers. That's the importance of the fact that Asia is too big to dominate, even for China. It could also unite the United States, Europe, and Japan into a tighter economic alliance designed to protect free-market capitalism from China's state capitalist expansion.

China is unlikely to fare as well in this scenario as the Soviet Union did, because domestic priorities will probably ensure that it is simply too expensive for Beijing to build a Soviet-scale global military presence, and because China has nothing like the ideological and cultural appeal that the Soviet Union once held for many in the developing world. China has earned a lot of friends within cash-hungry governments in both the established and the emerging worlds, but it has little chance of capturing the hearts and minds of

---

* More than a million Taiwanese now live on the mainland.

the people who live in these countries. The United States would also lack some of its advantages of the last century. Without the kind of unity imposed by the aftermath of World War II, there will not be a new Bretton Woods to align countries' economic policies, no Washington Consensus that gives the United States global institutional dominance, no hunger in the rest of the world for U.S. exports or investment, and nothing like the ideological appeal that came from the thirst for democracy after years of fascist dictatorship or fear of a Soviet advance. To be sure, Cold War 2.0 is more likely to emerge than either the G2 or concert scenarios, but many factors limit the risk of a direct and destabilizing U.S.-Chinese conflict.

A WORLD OF REGIONS—TO EACH HIS OWN

Our fourth scenario is a world without global leadership, one in which many of the rest will rise, but only to tackle local and regional issues. The United States remains the world's only truly global military power, but the growing economic muscle and technological sophistication of rising powers limit the importance of this advantage. This is a world where regional leaders provide some public goods within their respective spheres of influence, while increasingly self-confident regional heavyweights largely ignore major multinational institutions. This is for now the most likely of the post-G-Zero scenarios, because it requires no compromises among powerful states, no leaps of faith on global problem solving—and because it appears to be the path that the world is already on.

The phenomenon is worldwide but plays out differently in each region. Europe and Latin America are far more cooperative and institutionalized than Asia or Africa. That difference will only grow. European and Latin American states are more likely to accept leadership from Germany and Brazil than Asian or former Soviet states are to welcome Chinese or Russian hegemony. And although African institutions, both for commerce and peacekeeping, are stronger than they used to be, they still have a long way to go. In short, some regions will prove more naturally cohesive than others. Some would-be local powers will have to rely more often on coercion. Others can use common ethnic or religious ties to build informal coalitions of like-minded governments. With so many different potential patterns of development, each region deserves a closer look.

Begin with the Arab world. The political earthquakes in North Africa and the Middle East in 2011 ravaged governments in Egypt, Tunisia, Libya, and Yemen. Only in Libya did the United States and NATO play a crucial role in this historic shift—and only after an appeal from other Arab governments. In response to both the threat of revolutionary contagion and the inability and unwillingness of outside powers to limit its spread, regional powerhouse Saudi Arabia moved to use its leadership of the Gulf Cooperation Council to bolster Arab monarchies. In May 2011, Riyadh looked to extend its reach by formally inviting Jordan and Morocco to join the club. These countries have powerful motivations for a new level of cooperation: They are threatened both by Iran's growing regional power and by fears of further public unrest, and anxious over the diminished U.S. role in the Middle East. With the Saudis playing the largest role in coordinating policy and keeping the peace, the GCC could move more quickly toward a common currency, deeper trade and investment ties, and much closer cooperation on foreign and security policy.[14] That will help preserve stability in the Gulf, but the G-Zero will allow sectarianism in places like Iraq and Syria to generate new problems elsewhere in the Middle East. Even states outside the Gulf like Morocco, Algeria, and Jordan could face new challenges in years ahead. Recently, Saudi Arabia has even mentioned political union within the GCC. While implementation is unrealistic for the foreseeable future, Riyadh's diplomacy alone—and the fact that other states have been receptive to it in theory—hints at ideological consolidation.

In Europe, a growing sense of crisis in the creditworthiness of several European countries has left cash-rich Germany in an enhanced regional leadership role—whether German officials and taxpayers like it or not. Berlin will be crucial to any plan to reform the Eurozone, the Schengen Agreement on borders, or the European Union itself. But if Europe can forge agreements among member states that combine a new commitment to the single currency with much closer coordination on state spending and tax policies, the continent will emerge as the world's most effective and efficiently run region. We're still extremely unlikely to see a single European foreign and defense policy—combining harmonization of fiscal policy with monetary union will absorb virtually all of Europe's time and attention in years to come—but with more obvious German leadership, Europe could serve as a model for other regions. In fact, Saudi Arabia and Germany are strong examples of the kinds of local powers most likely to fill regional vacuums created by America's more frugal foreign policy and the inability of multinational institutions to meet emerging challenges with credible solutions.

What role might Britain play in this German-led Europe? As a member of the European Union that has chosen not to adopt the euro, the United Kingdom has long kept one foot on the continent and one foot outside it. Having refused to surrender control of its monetary policy to the European Central Bank, Britain is equally unlikely to cede effective control of its ability to set tax and spending levels. That's why a much more tightly consolidated Europe will probably push Britain closer to its English-speaking cousins in North America, a region that will continue to be dominated by the United States.

In South America, there remains a philosophical divide on economic policy among countries like Brazil, Chile, Peru, and Colombia, which have welcomed foreign investment in many sectors and worked to keep inflation in check, and those like Venezuela, Ecuador, and Bolivia, which have taken a more arbitrary, populist approach to development. Brazil's bid to lift millions toward the middle class without bankrupting the country is the wave of the future in Latin America, and as that nation establishes greater dominance across the region, more states are likely to follow its example. The region's relative peace will bolster its prosperity, and some Central American economies may decide that they prefer Brasília's orbit to Washington's.

Given its ability to pivot, we can expect Africa to continue to grow its urban middle class and its purchasing power. But this is not a region where we can expect the level of coordination we see in Europe—or even in Southeast Asia or Latin America. Africa is more likely to divide into subregions with countries like Nigeria, South Africa, and Kenya leading greater local economic integration while many other governments contribute to leadership on particular issues of interest, from conflict resolution to peacekeeping and from new trade ties to new deals on collective security.

If Russia can develop and diversify its domestic economy, or if oil prices remain high enough to continue to fill Russian coffers with cash, Moscow should be able to build greater political and economic influence across much of the territory of the former Soviet Union. Kazakhstan will keep the ability to pivot, but states like Ukraine and Georgia that prefer closer ties with Europe will remain in Russia's shadow. In this region, as in the Middle East, local success and stability will depend heavily on the international price of crude oil and natural gas.

Asia will remain the most volatile region. China, India, and Japan are highly unlikely to happily coexist for long, and states like Indonesia, South Korea, and Thailand are large enough to resist being pulled entirely into another country's orbit. Asia will probably enhance its role as the engine of global economic growth, but the region still has too many potential security emergencies.

A world of regions would not be without international cooperation. Should this scenario come to pass, expect to see small groups of established and emerging powers working together on issues of common interest. Brazil, Russia, India, China, and South Africa will continue to try to build on trade and investment ties in some areas and to increase their weight within lending institutions like the IMF and the World Bank. Russia and China will use organizations like the Shanghai Cooperation Organization to bolster their regional influence and to keep the United States from deepening ties with other members. Developing states in Latin America and Africa, led by Brazil and South Africa, will work to further develop "south-south" political and commercial relations. America, Europe, and China will continue to depend on the bilateral trade relationships they have established. But this more fragmented international order will be without global leadership and a first provider of global public goods.

Pivot states are liable to be even more successful in this scenario. No global conflict will force them to choose sides, and the lack of multilateral agreements on trade, investment, standards, and other issues will provide states flexible enough to take advantage with opportunities to form one-on-one relations with multiple other governments, playing one off another to secure the most profitable terms of engagement. The most intriguing pivot-state-related question will be whether Europe remains a coherent enough political and economic entity to effectively pivot between America and China or whether the continent will fragment, leaving Germany to enjoy this advantage on its own. Strong states that fall between regions—like Turkey, Egypt, and Kazakhstan—will have similar opportunities.

SCENARIO X—THE G-SUBZERO

Given the various forms of turmoil the G-Zero is likely to create, one other post-G-Zero possibility deserves consideration. It's a wild-card scenario, one that threatens a very different kind of fragmentation of the international order. A generation ago, some predicted that the increasingly free flow of ideas, information, people, money, goods, and services would undermine the power of national governments to maintain firm control of political and economic policy, perhaps even rendering states all but irrelevant. That didn't happen, in part because some emerging-market governments used state dominance of commerce to ensure that they controlled a large enough share of market wealth to enhance their political control. The financial crisis gave states even greater incentives to double down on that strategy. It's possible that the potential upheaval created by the lack of international leadership during the G-Zero era will further strengthen the state.

But what if it doesn't? What if, instead of empowering the state to protect citizens from crisis, the G-Zero creates the kinds of problems that discredit the state, cripple its credibility, and arouse enough public anger that citizens look for alternatives? In fact, there are many ways in which central governments could lose much of their power, especially to local-level power brokers. The subtlest form of this trend might be a willingness by midlevel officials or local governments to ignore central government rules, plans, and policies and to substitute their own. Mikhail Gorbachev's earliest efforts to reform the Soviet state came to almost nothing, in part because officials within the bureaucracy, anxious to protect the privileges that the system provided them, simply ignored many orders from above. The system itself fought back against efforts to change it. Gorbachev then turned to a policy known as glasnost (openness) to bypass much of the bureaucracy and appeal directly for public support for his plans. The Soviet system then collapsed because openness soon unleashed the centrifugal forces that pulled the empire apart.

Today's China is in need of long-term economic and social reforms almost as ambitious, and its government will be undertaking these changes just at a time when the G-Zero is likely to supply the system with unexpected shocks. If Beijing can't manage the growing social unrest described in the previous chapter, if it can't cope with a rising tide of environmental disasters, if global rebalancing begins to cost China jobs and to benefit neighboring economies at China's expense, if a more serious market meltdown inside Europe and the United States—China's leading trade partners—puts tens of millions out of work, if public disgust with corruption takes on a life of its own on the Internet, if state attempts to quell another student uprising meet resistance coordinated with modern tools of communication, we might well see a fundamental change over time in how China is actually governed. It doesn't take the collapse of the state or a revolution to bring about this change. But if lower-level state bureaucrats and local officials decide to run their own agendas, and if Beijing is unable to implement the plans it makes, China's central government could remain much too preoccupied managing domestic challenges to play any important role on the international stage.

Another "what if": What if, instead of bringing Europe closer together, debt crises pull the continent apart? Several countries withdraw from the euro. The European Union itself fragments. Debt burdens deprive federal governments of the resources they need to create and enforce policy. Local governments usurp much of their authority, leading to fragmentation of power within states like Italy and France. That breakdown is then exacerbated by the reemergence of separatist movements in Britain, Belgium, and Spain. This phenomenon then spreads to regions where borders have historically been drawn by outsiders. Local governments in the Caucasus region and Central Asia point to international recognition of independence for Kosovo as a precedent for small ethnically based states to declare independence. Former European colonies in Africa, including large resource-rich states like Nigeria and the Democratic Republic of Congo, face greater internal stresses as local governments insist on greater control over natural wealth drawn from within "their" territories.

This is the relatively benign version of the wild-card scenario. What about states that depend for their stability on the revenue generated by the export of crude oil? For the next several decades, the world will continue to rely for a substantial percentage of its energy needs on oil and natural gas, but over time, other fuel sources will become more affordable, plentiful, and easier to use.

For all the talk in America about reducing U.S. dependence on Saudi oil, no one is more dependent on Saudi oil than the royal family of Saudi Arabia. What happens to political stability on the Arabian Peninsula when Saudi oil is a much smaller part of the world's fuel mix? Can the Saudis diversify their economy quickly enough when technological changes in fuel production reach a tipping point? Oil- and gas-rich Iran might face a similar generational challenge.

How about Venezuela, a country where a throwback populist government uses its (declining) oil revenues to pay for just about everything the Venezuelan people need to import? Leaving aside the question of separatist pressures, what happens in Nigeria, West Africa's primary source of stability, if crude prices fall sharply? Thanks to its banking and consumer sectors, Nigeria is not nearly as reliant on oil as it used to be. But oil revenue and the advantages it provides the country's central government have played a critical role in maintaining the delicate balance inside Nigeria between the Muslim provinces of the north, the Christian provinces of the south, the restive communities of the oil-rich Niger Delta, and all the local and tribal differences within each of these regions.

Today, Russia has a strong central government, but its popularity and baseline legitimacy depend largely on one man: Vladimir Putin. This is a country that encompasses 170 different ethnic groups and dozens of minority languages, across eighty-nine regions covering eight time zones and one-seventh of the earth's land surface. The history of the Russian Empire, then the Soviet Union, is one of shifting borders. If its oil and natural gas become a lot less valuable before the Russian government and its business community can much more fully diversify the country's economy, the Russian government may one day find itself with far too many internal challenges even to dominate its own citizens, never mind its neighbors. In fact, Putin's 2012 election bid has triggered angry demonstrations that took the media (and Putin) by surprise.

Strife within so many important countries could inflict considerable damage on the global economy, with dire consequences for volatile and vulnerable states like Pakistan, which relies on Saudi, U.S., and Chinese help to keep its government afloat. Globalization faces a fundamental setback as global supply chains become unmanageable and a lot more borders appear *within* states. Local actors refuse to respect agreements signed at the national level that exploit their resources. In some cases, they seize assets and property owned by the state (pipelines, reservoirs, ports) or by companies based beyond their borders. This issue could also allow local political opportunists to exploit divisions of various kinds within states like Iraq, Syria, and the former Soviet republics of the Caucasus and Central Asia—states whose borders were established by outsiders ignorant of older ethnic, sectarian, and tribal boundaries or willing to ignore them for reasons of their own.

What happens if political collapse in some of these states leads not to new government but to no government? The international community might not be able to cope with all the threats that state failure could create. State failure in Somalia or Yemen is one thing. That kind of breakdown in Pakistan or Russia is quite another. Then there is the subtler version of this issue. In countries like India and Brazil, large populations of the urban poor living in largely ungoverned enclaves might simply provide their own governance, neighborhood by neighborhood, with an informal economy that operates under its own rules. This is a phenomenon already developing in some of the world's most important emerging cities.[15]

Call this larger scenario the G-Subzero. As leadership weakens and power fragments inside individual countries, control is divided between local and central leaders, and competition arises among power brokers within individual states. In China and Russia, cash-rich governments maintain control of the troops and guns needed to maintain basic order, but other states could face more existential threats.

A lesson of the terrorism-plagued first decade of the twenty-first century is that ungoverned places can become breeding grounds for all sorts of trouble. Militant fanaticism is just one issue. Food shortages, criminal gangs, large-scale drug trafficking, and public health crises transmitted across borders add to the list. If the leaderless G-Zero era in international politics generates global problems that metastasize into a thousand local emergencies, large parts of important countries could go ungoverned—or become ungovernable. And that result would ensure that whatever the balance of power among the world's most powerful states, they could all find themselves fully occupied with management of internal crises.

This is without question the lowest probability of all the scenarios detailed here. For the moment, most states are able to maintain a healthy enough balance of power between central and local officials and between the state and its constituents to provide basic security and to generate opportunities for most citizens—even if in some countries those opportunities do not include the right to play an independent and important role in the country's political decision making. But the longer the G-Zero lasts, the more likely this scenario becomes.

* * *

Finally, we turn to the question of what can be done to minimize the damage that a leaderless international order might inflict and to prepare for what comes next, as policymakers in Washington face an increasingly unpredictable landscape.

CHAPTER SIX

G-Zero America

We have it in our power to begin the world over again.
—Thomas Paine, *Common Sense*

There are *always* second acts in American life.

Anyone who believes that American decline is inevitable has chosen to ignore the history of the United States and its people. Yes, the world has changed. America cannot lead as it did during the second half of the twentieth century, because the global balance of power has shifted profoundly since the Allies gathered at Bretton Woods in 1944. But the country's underlying strengths ensure that if Americans can rebuild power from within during this era of rebalancing at home and abroad, U.S. leadership can again prove crucial for international peace and prosperity. The unstable character of the G-Zero ensures that it cannot last, and leadership in a *post*-G-Zero world should be the goal that guides American foreign and domestic policies in years to come.

For the moment, pessimism prevails.[1] Confidence in U.S. economic resilience lies buried beneath a mountain of debt. Washington must adopt a more cost-sensitive approach to foreign and defense policy, and the rest of the world knows it. The U.S. system of primary and secondary education is not preparing a new generation of students to compete, particularly in math and science, or even to go to college.* Physical infrastructure is in bad shape, too. Many of America's schools, hospitals, roads, bridges, ports, and airports have fallen into disrepair.† Fixing all these problems will require a level of cooperation between Democrats and Republicans that for the moment appears laughably unlikely.

Yet beneath all this erosion lies a solid foundation for American revival. Despite necessary cutbacks in defense spending, Washington will continue to invest far more money in hard power than any potential rival can afford to match. That alone will ensure that America remains a sought-after security partner, particularly if the rise of regional powers persuades smaller states to look to the United States for protection. America's soft power will also remain a priceless national asset. Mandarin Chinese is not going to replace English as the world's most popular second language. Nor can any individual country eclipse America's cultural appeal or offer a competing political or socioeconomic ideology, as the Soviet Union did during the Cold War. In addition, despite all the recent economic damage done by Washington's failure to effectively regulate its financial sector, intelligently governed free-market capitalism remains the world's only reliable engine of lasting prosperity.

---

* Between 1995 and 2008, the United States fell from second to thirteenth among OECD countries in the percentage of its citizens with college degrees.

† Between 2001 and 2011, the United States fell from seventh to twenty-third on the World Economic Forum's rankings of infrastructure quality.

Entrepreneurialism is and will remain a foundational American value and a core American strength.

For all its challenges, the resilience of American democracy and the transparency of its governing institutions continue to inspire those in the developing world who have no say in how they are governed. Each generation offers new reminders that authoritarian governments will always be brittle. They can maintain the illusion of solidity for years, even decades. But when they fall, as we saw across Eastern Europe in 1989 and North Africa in 2011, they can collapse with stunning speed. The emerging world's democracies are much more likely to withstand the test of time in their present form, but even India, Brazil, and Turkey will face serious institutional tests in years to come if the G-Zero generates the kinds of problems that shock their still-developing economies.

That said, and despite America's underlying strengths, G-Zero will impose new limits on Washington's choices. The most immediate question facing U.S. policymakers will be how to maintain domestic support for protection of the country's critical foreign policy interests, even as the country's international status takes a hit. Intense political focus on the federal debt and the long wars in Afghanistan and Iraq have stoked public demand for a more sharply reduced U.S. role in the world than at any time since the attack on Pearl Harbor. A survey of "long-range foreign policy priorities" conducted by the Pew Research Center in May 2011 found that the only goals winning majority support from U.S. respondents were protection of jobs, protection of the United States from terrorist attacks, and reduction of U.S. dependence on imported energy. The percentage of those surveyed who favored "reducing U.S. military commitments overseas" surged from 26 percent in September 2001 to 46 percent in May 2011. "Promoting democracy abroad" won support from just 13 percent of respondents, and nearly half said that the United States "should mind its own business internationally."[2]

Nor can Washington look to its NATO allies for help with the heavy lifting. European defense spending fell by 15 percent in the decade that followed the September 11 terrorist attacks, and budget crises in several European countries threaten an even steeper drop in years to come. The global economic volatility and growth in the intensity of regional conflicts, particularly in Asia and the Middle East, are certain to further dampen the enthusiasm of both American voters and American allies for costly foreign interventions. That's a lot for political officials to overcome in arguing against a new isolationism, but it's exactly what's needed if America is to begin preparing for the post-G-Zero world.

LESSONS FROM WINNERS AND LOSERS

With so many factors weighing on the country's self-confidence, how can America rebuild for the post-G-Zero world? The best answers can be found in our forecasts of the G-Zero era's winners and losers. Whether countries or companies, losers tend to resist or ignore changes in the world around them. They operate in a wished-for world, live beyond their means, and refuse to share costs or to accept others' rules. Winners accept the world as it is. They set aside vanity, learn from their mistakes, adapt to changing circumstances, innovate where possible, partner when necessary, and play to their core strengths.

Setting aside vanity means accepting that American-imposed solutions are not always best. Not every developing country is ready for multiparty democracy and large-scale privatization of a tightly controlled economy. U.S. policymakers must do more than simply say they understand this. They must prove it by allowing for local solutions to local problems. Learning from mistakes means accepting that deficits matter, that compromise is a virtue, and that even a colossus must live within its means. Adapting to changing circumstances means avoiding doctrinaire approaches to the country's challenges. Emerging stronger from the G-Zero will require innovative approaches to issues such as energy security, the growth of cyberthreats, nuclear proliferation, terrorism, and climate change—and it will require Washington to maximize its strength by partnering with an ever-shifting constellation of potential allies on each of these individual tests.

Most of all, Americans should have faith in their country's core strengths. Lasting power comes from within. The primary goal of American policymakers should be to bolster the nation's security by sharply reducing its debt burden—no reform that fails to trim the fat from America's sacred cows can accomplish this goal. Most Republicans want to cut the spiraling costs of America's largest entitlement programs, particularly Social Security and Medicare, and reduce government spending in many other areas. But they oppose substantive cuts in military spending and vow not to raise taxes on a single American. Most Democrats want to help rebalance the books by increasing taxes, particularly on the wealthiest Americans, and significantly reduce defense spending. They want to stimulate the next round of U.S. economic growth with a surge in state spending on the kinds of infrastructure projects that create large numbers of jobs and enhance the country's long-term competitiveness. At the same time, they resolutely oppose any meaningful reduction in pension and health benefits.

This reality makes clear that, even in America, failure is an option. Nothing is inevitable about a U.S. revival. If too many lawmakers hold to the idea that the political needs of the moment can always trump long-term investment in the country's future, if they act as though absolute fidelity to party orthodoxy is a cardinal virtue and that compromise amounts to a failure of will, we can expect lasting, perhaps permanent damage to America's political self-confidence and economic dynamism.

The good news is that, just as the G-Zero will create crises that might force international cooperation where none existed before, tough economic times in the United States have put issues once considered beyond politics squarely on the bargaining table. Each side can give the other cover to make unpopular choices, especially if voters, disgusted with petty partisan politics, force them to do it. Americans will have to pay higher taxes, delay retirement, accept smaller pensions, and enjoy less generous health care benefits.

It may take a viable third-party alternative or, more likely, a deeper sense of national crisis to push the country toward compromise, but a critical mass of Democrats and Republicans is much more likely to accept painful sacrifices if voters with no enduring loyalty to either party punish those who ignore the need for comprehensive change. Without this national rebalancing, the United States will emerge from the G-Zero with less strength, less confidence, a lower standard of living, and less to offer the rest of the world.

American foreign policy must reflect this need to restore the country's economic vitality. President Obama has drawn intense fire from political rivals for his refusal to commit to a consistent foreign policy doctrine and for his willingness to "lead from behind." But G-Zero America can't afford to lead the charge into every battle, and it doesn't need a foreign policy doctrine that allows U.S. allies and enemies to anticipate how Washington will respond to a hypothetical set of circumstances. Instead, U.S. policymakers need a consistent set of broad principles that guide their actions—

one of which should be attention to cost—and the flexibility to adapt to each unique set of circumstances. An ideologically driven foreign policy is a luxury that G-Zero America cannot afford.

Lawmakers will have to do more with less, and defense cuts will be necessary. Though America has had no post–Cold War superpower rival, U.S. defense spending rose every year from 1998 to 2010. Former Reagan administration Pentagon official Lawrence Korb has argued that a cut of as much as $1 trillion over the next ten to twelve years would not undermine U.S. national security.[3] G-Zero America cannot afford to station troops where none are needed or to invest billions in weapons designed to win twentieth-century wars. The need to carefully weigh costs and benefits will become a fact of daily life. When defense cuts have been made in the past, politics has too often proven the deciding factor in what is cut and by how much.

To win support from key lawmakers, the pain associated with base closings, personnel cuts, and scaled-back defense contracts has been spread as widely and thinly as possible—though the most influential lawmakers are often allowed to protect their constituents at the expense of others. It is not realistic (or desirable) to expect members of Congress to ignore the needs of their states and districts, particularly in a time of economic hardship, but in the interest of the country's defense, cuts should be guided mainly by the long-term strategic calculations of military planners, not the immediate political needs of local lawmakers. It is not for those of us with limited knowledge of these questions to single out particular bases or weapons systems for cuts. Instead, we can urge those who will make these decisions to recognize that in a G-Zero world, regional conflicts are the most likely—particularly in Asia—and economic tools and cyberweapons will often be used by those who can't win a war fought with planes, tanks, and troops.

Policymakers should also recognize that even in a G-Zero world, circumstance will sometimes provide Washington with valuable opportunities for cost-effective leadership. To its credit, the Obama administration took full advantage of one such opportunity in 2011. Having alienated virtually everyone outside his country, Libyan strongman Muammar Gadhafi took to the radio one February evening to alert the citizens of Benghazi, in the east of the country, that his soldiers were advancing on the city in search of rebels. "Prepare yourselves for tonight. We will find you in your closets," he warned. Fearing that Gadhafi was about to massacre huge numbers of his own people, the Arab League called for establishment of a no-fly zone over the country. The United States and its European allies seized the opportunity to push Resolution 1973 through the UN Security Council, a declaration that allowed Western powers to use "all necessary measures" to protect the Libyan people.[4] That proved a broad enough mandate to allow NATO the political cover it needed to eventually bomb Gadhafi from power.

In the end, a combination of diplomatic support from the Arab League, determined (if amateurish) Libyan rebels, and America's NATO allies allowed the United States to act as leader of last resort. Washington assumed too much of the financial cost, but mass murder was averted, allies did much of the bombing, Libyans did all the on-the-ground fighting,[*] and Gadhafi was defeated and killed without the loss of a single American life.

Such circumstances are rare. Intervention would not have been possible in support of the protests in Iran that followed that country's disputed 2009 presidential election, and it would not have been welcome in Egypt during the uprising that eventually ousted President Hosni Mubarak in 2011. In both cases, it was important, espe-

---

[*]   At least on the rebels' side. Gadhafi employed mercenaries from several other African countries.

cially to the protesters themselves, that challenges to state power were mounted by locals, not foreigners. The kinds of long-term occupations we've seen in Iraq and Afghanistan will be prohibitively expensive for years to come, but given U.S. military power, even assuming substantial cuts are made, Americans will have more opportunities to provide global public goods. It's important to seize as many of them as possible, because if America is to play a leading role in shaping the post-G-Zero order, Washington must continue to feed international demand for U.S. leadership.

REINVEST IN GLOBALIZATION

Finally, no foreign policy tool is more cost-effective than an intelligently negotiated free trade agreement. Trade will be crucial for both the reinvigoration of America's economy and the success of U.S. foreign policy, during the G-Zero era and beyond. Nowhere are trade ties more important than in Asia, the region with greatest potential for both commerce and conflict. As we have seen, tensions are growing across Asia as many countries feel they must choose between security ties with the United States and deepening economic relations with China. Beijing, aware of this tension, is doing its best to ensure that trade carries the day.

China has signed a number of lucrative trade deals in recent years, including a landmark agreement with the Association of Southeast Asian Nations (ASEAN), which went into effect in early 2010 with six of the member nations.* The China-ASEAN free trade agreement is now the world's third largest by total trade value, and it covers an area that includes 1.9 billion people. Counting each

---

* The remaining four nations will be phased in by 2015.

ASEAN country individually, China now has seventeen trade agreements in place, including thirteen in Asia, and ASEAN's trade with China grew from $32 billion in 2000 to more than $250 billion in 2010.

Beijing's motives are not simply commercial. It is wisely integrating China ever more deeply into Asian politics, giving its neighbors a direct stake in China's rise and reducing the importance of America, Europe, and Japan for the economies of Indonesia, Thailand, Singapore, Vietnam, and the Philippines. America, in particular, is missing out on new opportunities. The U.S. share of Asian trade fell from 35 percent in 1990 to just 18 percent in 2008. Washington cannot afford to be pushed from Asia if it is to revitalize the U.S. economy and to influence the evolution of the world's most important and potentially volatile region. This is why the Obama administration has devoted so much energy to promoting the Trans-Pacific Partnership, a process that includes Australia, Brunei, Chile, Malaysia, New Zealand, Peru, Singapore, Vietnam, and the United States. Japan has indicated an interest in joining negotiations. China is notably absent.

The most important reason for Washington to reinvest in trade is that this is the playing field on which America performs at its best. The past several decades have taught us that the United States is far from the only country that profits from the free flow of ideas, information, people, money, goods, and services. All those political, economic, and cultural strengths that make America an exceptional power offer the greatest advantage in an arena of open competition. If the G-Zero becomes an era of new walls and new restrictions, Americans will be forced to compete in someone else's game. But if the future is determined by the power to invent, innovate, streamline, brand, and sell, America will be tough to beat.

In the meantime, Washington must accept the limits of U.S.

leadership in a G-Zero world. Americans must turn their backs on commitments that can't be sustained and rebuild the nation's strength from within. They must remain engaged with the world wherever vital national interests are at stake and look for cost-effective ways to maintain international demand for U.S. leadership. If farsighted U.S. policymakers can use this period of transition to deepen traditional alliances, those based on both shared values and shared interests, and seek out new partners and new allies, they will have taken a crucial step toward making America indispensable for the world that comes next.

ACKNOWLEDGMENTS

Most books should be essays. Most essays, op-eds. Most op-eds, blog posts. Most blog posts, tweets. And most tweets should never have been tweeted.

Book writing feels even more audacious than hope these days—there's just so much out there. So first, thanks to you, my reader. You've gotten this far and I am deeply grateful. I hope you think *Every Nation for Itself* proves a clear exception to the rule.

If it is, it's because I've benefited from all sorts of brilliant folks helping me figure out which end is up. My gratitude to all my friends and colleagues willing to listen to my thoughts and improve upon them: Peter Apps, Matthew Bishop, Vint Cerf, Steve Clemons, Jared Cohen, Sam DiPiazza, Catherine Fieschi, Chrystia Freeland, David Fromkin, Martina Gmur, Ken Griffin, Nikolas Gvosdev, Guy Hands, Ken Hersh, Zachary Karabell, Tom Keene, Parag Khanna, Sallie Krawcheck, Dan and Eric Loeb (no relation), Steve Mann, Maziar Minovi, Bijan Mossavar-Rahmani, Nader Mousavizadeh, Martin Nagele, Mary Pang, Niko Pfund, Juan Pujadas, Gideon Rachman, Doug and Heidi Rediker, Joel Rosenthal, Marci Shore, Doug Shuman, Martin Sorrell, Larry Summers, Nick Thompson, Enzo Viscusi, Fareed Zakaria, and Bob Zoellick.

Nouriel Roubini has been my confederate for about a decade. We're an odd couple in disposition. Nouriel sees a glass that's mostly empty; I'm just happy there's any water in the glass at all. I bounced the G-Zero off him before I started writing the book, and we wrote an essay last year together to get folks talking about it (further thanks to *Foreign Affairs*' then–newly appointed editor Gideon Rose for rushing it through the process!). My deep appreciation to him.

I'm fortunate to count David Gordon among my best friends. He's brilliant, balanced, and a thoroughly lovely human being. When I initially broached the idea of the G-Zero, we spent weeks arguing over (er, discussing loudly) the implications. David has ended up informing my thinking of the world in countless ways, hopefully stirring up a bit of trouble in the process. His advice and commentary have been invaluable.

It's been nearly fifteen years since I started Eurasia Group, now a burgeoning archipelago of wayward political scientists. Along with David, I'm fortunate to work with friends, many of whom I've known since I was still in school. It's honest, clean fun. They know my foibles, and they call me out when I'm being difficult. Or when I'm wrong.

That starts with the backbone of Eurasia Group—our research team. They're wonderful, and they've made an enormous difference in my writing. My thanks to all of them here: Dan Alamariu, Erasto Almeida, Antonio Barroso, Allyson Benton, Heather Berkman, Aditya Bhattacharji, Alex Brideau, Shamila Chaudhary, Carroll Colley, Nick Consonery, Patrick Cullen, Daniil Davydoff, Philippe de Pontet, Seema Desai, James Fallon, Evan Feigenbaum, Gemma Ferst, Helen Fessenden, Jeff Finch, James Clinton Francis,

Anne Fruhauf, Iku Fujimatsu, Chris Garman, Nitzan Goldberger, Jeremy Gordon, Risa Grais-Targow, John Green, Samantha Grenville, Stephanie Haffner, Crispin Hawes, Bob Herrera-Lim, Emily Hoch, Robert Johnston, Filipa Jorge, Ayham Kamel, Jesse Kaplan, Daniel Kerner, Famke Krumbmuller, Cliff Kupchan, Jennifer Lee, Shaun Levine, Yael Levine, Damien Ma, Courtney Rickert McCaffrey, Aditi Marisetti, Naz Masraff, Michal Meidan, Marc Mercer, Jun Okumura, Leslie Palti-Guzman, Will Pearson, Wolfango Piccoli, Greg Priddy, Mujtaba Rahman, Carlos Ramirez, Divya Reddy, Sasha Riser-Kositsky, Scott Rosenstein, Hani Sabra, Ross Schaap, Scott Seaman, Adam Siegel, Otilia Simkova, David Sloan, Jenia Ustinova, Christopher Walker, Sean West, and Jack Zhang.

Willis Sparks has worked with me for seven years and lord knows how many (four!) books now. He's irreplaceable. I absolutely adore working with him. It's becoming a surprisingly intuitive relationship; I've come to appreciate the way Willis's ideas extend and enrich mine. The absurdly young and talented Andrew Ross Sorkin gave me a call a year ago and said if I needed a crack researcher, he had just the guy. I hired Mike Sard pretty much on the spot. He's been a fantastic asset, and his research on this book has been indispensable. My deep thanks to them both.

They all have different day jobs at Eurasia Group, but when it comes to publicity, marketing, scheduling, and everything else involved in going from completed manuscript to book campaign, Jen Dixon, Emma Lindqvist, Alex Lloyd, and Jenna Rosebery are the A team. They're delightful and they "get it." It's a privilege to be working with all of them.

Not since my days as an academic have I actually published two books consecutively with the same editor. I hope that doesn't mean I'm impossible to work with. But I have greatly enjoyed working with Adrian Zackheim at Portfolio, who knows the business inside and out—and hasn't been shy making me aware of that. So too I've benefited from the unwavering enthusiasm and strategic vision of Portfolio's head of publicity, Allison McLean, and her colleague Jacquelynn Burke. I'd also like to thank my exceptionally talented and now veteran editor, Courtney Young, and our publicists, Angela Hayes and Lynn Goldberg, all of whom did such a fine job on *The End of the Free Market*. It's a pleasure to be engaged with all of them again.

Rafe Sagalyn had been persistently (and patiently) telling me that he should be my agent for something like five years. I finally listened. He's been a consummate professional. My appreciation to dearest Kirsten Sandberg for introducing us way back when.

So much for the audacity of book writing. As for hope, I have to admit that I love the idea of the G20. It would really be something if it worked. I'd also love a global climate deal and a new accord on free trade. And a pony. I hope you're listening, Santa.

New York
January 2012

NOTES

INTRODUCTION

1. The phrase "rise of the rest" was popularized by Fareed Zakaria in *The Post-American World* (New York: Norton, 2008).
2. Standard Chartered Bank, "The Super-Cycle Report," November 15, 2010, http://www.privatebank.standardchartered.com/_pdf/en/The%20 Super-cycle%20151110%20CB.pdf.

CHAPTER ONE: What Is the G-Zero?

1. Allegra Stratton and Jonathan Watts, "Mugabe and the Queen," *Guardian,* December 17, 2009, http://www.guardian.co.uk/environment/2009/ dec/17/copenhagen-gala-dinner.
2. "Endeavors to Build Global Hope: Chinese Premier's 60 Hours in Copenhagen," China View, December 25, 2009, http://news.xinhuanet .com/english/2009-12/25/content_12701355.htm.
3. Tobias Rapp, Christian Schwägerl, and Gerald Traufetter, "The Cophenhagen Protocol: How China and India Sabotaged the UN Climate Summit," *Spiegel Online,* May 5, 2010, http://www.spiegel.de/interna tional/world/0,1518,692861,00.html.

4. Michael Mandelbaum, *The Frugal Superpower: America's Global Leadership in a Cash-Strapped Era* (New York: PublicAffairs, 2010), 21.

5. Keith Bradsher, "China Grows More Picky about Debt," *New York Times,* May 20, 2009, http://www.nytimes.com/2009/05/21/business/global/21reserves.html?pagewanted=all.

6. Forrest Jones, "Roach: China May Stop Buying U.S. Debt," Money News.com, August 19, 2011, http://www.moneynews.com/Economy/China-U-S-Treasurys-StephenRoach/2011/08/19/id/407995.

7. A CNN poll of American adults from August 2011 ranked the economy as "the most important issue facing the country today." "Iraq, Afghanistan, and Libya" was the highest international issue, with just 5 percent. "Problems and Priorities," PollingReport.com, http://www.polling report.com/prioriti.htm.

8. By early 2011, just 3 percent of Americans viewed globalization as a good thing; 53 percent believed that free trade has hurt the nation overall (up from 46 percent in 2007, and 30 percent in 1999). Dustin Ensinger, "Globalization Increasingly Viewed as a Bad Thing," *Economy in Crisis,* January 28, 2011, http://economyincrisis.org/content/globalization-increasingly-viewed-bad-thing.

9. A June 25–26, 2011, Gallup poll found that 72 percent of Americans were in favor of—and just 23 percent opposed—Obama's announcement to withdraw 10,000 troops by the end of 2011, 20,000 more by the end of summer 2012, and the remainder by the end of 2014. Lydia Saad, "Americans Broadly Favor Obama's Afghanistan Pullout Plan," Gallup, June 29, 2011, http://www.gallup.com/poll/148313/Americans-Broadly-Favor-Obama-Afghanistan-Pullout-Plan.aspx.

10. Alex Crippen, "Transcript: Warren Buffett Tells Charlie Rose Why Congress Should Stop 'Coddling' the Super-Rich," *Warren Buffett Watch,* CNBC.com, August 17, 2011, http://www.cnbc.com/id/44174056/page/3/.

11. Helen Pidd, "German Media Fuels Public Resentment over Greek Bailout," *Guardian,* June 21, 2011, http://www.guardian.co.uk/world/2011/jun/21/german-media-bild-greece-bailout-resentment.

12. "Another Project in Trouble," *Economist,* April 28, 2011, http://www.economist.com/node/18618525?story_id=18618525.

13. Kim Willsher, "Tunisian Migrants Squatting in Paris Building Refuse

to Leave," *Los Angeles Times,* May 4, 2011, http://articles.latimes
.com/2011/may/04/world/la-fg-france-tunisians-20110504.

14. Fred Bergsten, "We Should Listen to Beijing's Currency Idea," *Financial Times,* April 8, 2009, http://www.ft.com/intl/cms/s/0/7372bbd0-2470-11de-9a01-00144feabdc0.html#axzz1USrq5IBl.

15. "Getting to Know the Real China," statement by H.E. Wen Jiabao, Consulate General of the People's Republic of China, in San Francisco, September 25, 2010, http://sanfrancisco.chineseconsulate.org/eng/xw/t755674.htm.

16. International Monetary Fund, "World Outlook Economic Database," updated June 17, 2011, http://www.imf.org/external/pubs/ft/weo/2011/01/weodata/index.aspx.

17. "Hard Questions," *Economist,* June 9, 2011, http://www.economist.com/node/18802750.

18. "G20 Replaces G7 as the Most Important Global Forum on Economic Issues, Says Indian Finance Chief," World Economic Forum, http://www.weforum.org/news/g20-replaces-g7-most-important-global-forum-economic-issues-says-indian-finance-chief. Recent events have not dimmed these hopes for everyone. In 2011, ex–prime minister of Australia Kevin Rudd said, "In essence the G20 brings together critical global stakeholders who have a combined interest in sustaining the fabric of the future global order." "The Future of the G20," the Hon. Kevin Rudd MP, Australian Minister for Foreign Affairs, April 27, 2011, http://www.foreignminister.gov.au/speeches/2011/kr_sp_110427.html.

19. "IMF Succession: China Urges 'Democratic' Process," Asia One News, May 26, 2011, http://www.asiaone.com/News/Latest%2BNews/Asia/Story/A1Story20110526-280802.html.

20. "China Development Loans Beat World Bank, *FT* Says," *Hürriyet Daily News,* January 18, 2011, http://www.hurriyetdailynews.com/n.php?n=china-development-loans-beat-world-bank-ft-says-2011-01-18.

21. In 2008, Russian president Dmitry Medvedev pushed for a Russian sphere of influence. He explained, "Russia, like other countries in the world, has regions where it has privileged interests." This vague sphere would not be limited to Russia's immediate neighbors. Said Medvedev, "It is the border region, but not only." Andrew E. Kramer, "Russia Claims Its Sphere of Influence in the World," *New York Times,* August

31, 2008, http://www.nytimes.com/2008/09/01/world/europe/01russia
.html.

22. Bappa Majumdar, "BlackBerry Assures India on Access to Services,"
Reuters, August 13, 2010, http://www.reuters.com/article/2010/08/13/
us-blackberry-idUSTRE67151F20100813. "Saudi Arabia Orders Blackberry Ban Starting Friday," *Jakarta Post,* August 4, 2010, http://www
.thejakartapost.com/news/2010/08/04/saudi-arabia-orders-blackberry-
ban-starting-friday.html.

CHAPTER TWO: The Road to the G-Zero

1. Derek W. Urwin, *A Political History of Western Europe since 1945* (Essex,
UK: Pearson Education Limited, 1968 [5th ed., 1997]), 21–24.

2. William Manchester, *American Caesar: Douglas MacArthur, 1880–1964*
(New York: Little, Brown, 1978), 464–65.

3. Urwin, *A Political History of Western Europe since 1945,* 22.

4. William H. Chafe, *The Unfinished Journey: America since World War II*
(New York: Oxford University Press, 1986 [4th ed., 1999]), 36.

5. Robert Skidelsky, *John Maynard Keynes: Fighting for Britain, 1937–1946*
(London: Macmillan, 2000), 337.

6. Chafe, *The Unfinished Journey,* 8–10.

7. During the Great Depression, unemployment in the United States averaged 13.3 percent. By 1944, the unemployed percentage of the labor
force had dipped to its lowest level in U.S. economic history: 1.2 percent.
Christopher J. Tassava, "The American Economy during World
War II," EH.net, http://eh.net/encyclopedia/article/tassava.WWII.

8. Articles of Agreement, International Monetary Fund and International
Bank for Reconstruction and Development, United Nations Monetary
and Financial Conference, Bretton Woods, N.H., July 1 to 22, 1944
(Washington, DC: U.S. Treasury), http://fraser.stlouisfed.org/docs/
historical/martin/17_07_19440701.pdf.

9. IHOP Company Overview, http://www.ihop.com/index.php?option=
com_content&task=view&id=20&Itemid=5.

10. Joseph Stiglitz, *Globalization and Its Discontents* (New York: Norton,
2003).

11. United Nations Monetary and Financial Conference, statement by the

president, June 29, 1944, http://www.archive.org/stream/departmentof
stat1144unit/departmentofstat1144unit_djvu.txt.

12. Timothy Green, *Central Bank Gold Reserves: An Historical Perspective since 1845,* World Gold Council, Research Study No. 23 (November 1999), http://www.famguardian.org/Subjects/MoneyBanking/Federal Reserve/CentralBankGoldReserves.pdf.

13. Robin Broad, *Unequal Alliance: The World Bank, the International Monetary Fund, and the Philippines* (Berkeley: University of California Press, 1988).

14. The new limit was set at 15 percent, where it remains today. Dennis Leech, "Voting Power in the Governance of the International Monetary Fund," *Annals of Operations Research* 109 (2002): 375–97, http://www2 .lse.ac.uk/CPNSS/projects/VPP/VPPpdf/VPPPublications/VPP02_08 .pdf.

15. David A. Phillips, *Reforming the World Bank: Twenty Years of Trial and Error* (New York: Cambridge University Press, 2009), 16.

16. International Financial Statistics (IFS) database at the IMF, http:// www.imf.org/external/data.htm (subscription needed to access). Alternatively, Gauri Bhatia, "No Big Bargaining in Smoky Rooms for IMF Job: Lagarde," CNBC.com, June 8, 2011, http://www.cnbc.com/ id/43321459, pegs the U.S.-Europe share of votes at roughly half.

17. Chafe, *The Unfinished Journey,* 68.

18. Urwin, *A Political History of Western Europe since 1945,* 52–56.

19. Barry Eichengreen, *Exorbitant Privilege: The Rise and Fall of the Dollar* (New York: Oxford University Press, 2011), 48 (10 percent of the budget); Barry Eichengreen, *Lessons from the Marshall Plan,* prepared for the *2011 World Development Report,* April 2010, http://wdr2011.worldbank .org/sites/default/files/pdfs/WDR_2011_Case_Study_Marshall_Plan_ 1.pdf ($13 billion).

20. Urwin, *A Political History of Western Europe since 1945,* 52–56.

21. Ibid., 34.

22. "West Germany: Woe in the Wirtschaftswunder," *Time,* January 6, 1967, http://www.time.com/time/magazine/article/0,9171,843206-1,00 .html.

23. Manchester, *American Caesar,* 470–71.

24. Ibid., 469.

25. Daniel Yergin, *The Prize: The Epic Quest for Oil, Money, and Power* (New York: Simon & Schuster, 1992), 542.

26. Ibid.

27. David Pilling, "China at Number Two . . . and Counting," *Financial Times,* August 18, 2010, http://www.ft.com/intl/cms/s/0/e9d0f552-a963-11df-a6f2-00144feabdc0.html#axzz1XoiQpcAb.

28. Yergin, *The Prize,* 542, 545–46.

29. "Nixon Ends Bretton Woods International Monetary System," YouTube, http://www.youtube.com/watch?v=iRzrlQU6K1o.

30. Yergin, *The Prize,* 588–612, 634.

31. Ezra F. Vogel, *The Four Little Dragons: The Spread of Industrialization in East Asia* (Cambridge, MA: Harvard University Press, 1993), 9.

32. James Riedel, "Economic Development in East Asia: Doing What Comes Naturally?," in *Achieving Industrialization in East Asia,* ed. Helen Hughes (Cambridge: Cambridge University Press, 1988).

33. Vogel, *The Four Little Dragons,* 1.

34. Clyde H. Farnsworth, "4 Asian Economies Assailed," *New York Times,* November 27, 1978, http://www.nytimes.com/1987/11/27/business/4-asian-economies-assailed.html.

35. Vogel, *The Four Little Dragons,* 1–12.

36. Nicholas Lardy, "The Economic Rise of China: Threat or Opportunity?," Federal Reserve Bank of Cleveland, August 1, 2003, https://www.clevelandfed.org/Research/commentary/2003/0801.pdf.

37. Forecasts of the arc of China's rise vary greatly. It will become the world's largest economy by 2050 (per HSBC), 2040 (Deutsche Bank), 2030 (IIE, World Bank), 2027 (Goldman Sachs), or 2020 (Citi, PwC). Recently, the IMF declared that China will prevail as soon as 2016 (if we assess with purchasing power parity). Citibank's 2015 trading nation prediction: http://www.cnbc.com/id/43506564. HSBC, 2050: http://cnbusinessnews.com/hsbc-china-to-become-worlds-largest-economy-by-2050/. Deutsche Bank Research, 2040: https://www.dbresearch.com/PROD/DBR_INTERNET_EN-PROD/PROD0000000000230537.pdf. IIE, 2030: http://www.ndtv.com/article/business/china-set-to-beat-us-as-no-1-economy-by-2030-44912. World Bank, 2030: http://www.reuters.com/article/2011/03/23/worldbank-idUSH9E7EL00H20110323. Goldman Sachs, 2027: http://www.thisislondon.co.uk/standard-business/

article-23770626-china-will-be-the-worlds-biggest-economy-by-2027.do. Citigroup, 2020: http://www.cnbc.com/id/41775174/US_Will_Be_the_World_s_Third_Largest_Economy_Citi. PwC, 2020: http://www.dailytelegraph.com.au/business/chinese-economy-to-be-worlds-largest-by-2020/story-e6frez7r-1225822120372. IMF, 2016: http://www.imf.org/external/datamapper/index.php.

38. William J. Broad and David E. Sanger, "Worm Was Perfect for Sabotaging Centrifuges," *New York Times,* November 18, 2010, http://www.nytimes.com/2010/11/19/world/middleeast/19stuxnet.html?sq=stuxnet&st=cse&scp=2&pagewanted=print.

39. Neil MacFarquhar, "189 Nations Reaffirm Goal of Ban on Nuclear Weapons," *New York Times,* May 28, 2010, http://www.nytimes.com/2010/05/29/world/middleeast/29nuke.html.

40. While the IAEA acknowledged "concern about the Israeli nuclear capabilities" for the first time in 2010, it stopped short of confirming Israel's widely known nuclear status. The same memo also reminds us that the United States supplied Israel with the Soreq Nuclear Research Center in June 1960. A CIA document in 1974 said the following: "We believe that Israel already has produced and stockpiled a small number of fission weapons." *Israeli Nuclear Capabilities,* report by the director general, IAEA Board of Governors General Conference, September 3, 2010, http://www.iaea.org/About/Policy/GC/GC54/GC54Documents/English/gc54-14_en.pdf. *Special National Intelligence Estimate: Prospects for Further Proliferation of Nuclear Weapons,* August 23, 1974, http://www.gwu.edu/~nsarchiv/NSAEBB/NSAEBB240/snie.pdf.

41. "The Growing Appeal of Zero," *Economist,* June 16, 2011, http://www.economist.com/node/18836134.

42. China's urban employment grew from 190.4 million workers in 1995 to an estimated 256.4 million in 2003. Eswar Prasad, ed., *China's Growth and Integration into the World Economy: Prospects and Challenges,* Occasional Paper 232 (Washington, DC: International Monetary Fund, 2004), http://prasad.dyson.cornell.edu/doc/books/ChinasGrowthAndIntegrationWithTheWorldEconomy-ProspectsAndChallenges_IMFOP232_2004.pdf.

43. When Deng Xiaoping died in 1997, China's foreign-exchange reserves stood just below $140 billion. By 2004, they were estimated above $650

billion. Eswar Prasad and Shang-Jin Wei, "The Chinese Approach to Capital Inflows: Patterns and Possible Explanations," in *Capital Controls and Capital Flows in Emerging Economies: Policies, Practices, Consequences,* ed. Sebastian Edwards (Chicago: University of Chicago Press, 2007), http://prasad.dyson.cornell.edu/doc/PrasadWeiChinaKFLows NBERFinal.pdf.

44. Ian Bremmer, *The End of the Free Market: Who Wins the War between States and Corporations?* (New York: Portfolio, 2010).

45. Charles Riley, "China: U.S. Debt Fight 'Dangerously Irresponsible,'" CNN Money, July 29, 2011, http://money.cnn.com/2011/07/29/news/international/china_debt_ceiling/index.htm.

CHAPTER THREE: The G-Zero Impact

1. Airports Council International, http://www.airports.org/cda/aci_common/display/main/aci_content07_banners.jsp?zn=aci&cp=1_725_2___.

2. Mike M. Ahlers, "Napolitano Sees Chance to Set Global Standards in Airline Security," CNN.com, January 26, 2010, http://articles.cnn.com/2010-01-26/us/napolitano.security_1_napolitano-security-standards-privacy-issues?_s=PM:US.

3. Ming Jinwei, "China as a Global Market," Xinhua, April 27, 2011, http://news.xinhuanet.com/english2010/indepth/2011-04/25/c_13845135.htm.

4. South Korea announced it is expanding its cybercommand and opening a cyberwarfare school in 2012. It claims that North Korea is vastly expanding a cyberunit of its own. "South Korea Expands Cyber Defence," News24.com, July 1, 2011, http://www.news24.com/SciTech/News/South-Korea-expands-cyber-defence-20110701. "North Korea Hacker Threat Grows as Cyber Unit Grows: Defector," Reuters, June 1, 2011, http://www.reuters.com/article/2011/06/01/us-korea-north-hackers-idUSTRE7501U420110601.

5. "Person of the Year 2010," *Time,* December 15, 2011, http://www.time.com/time/specials/packages/article/0,28804,2036683_2037118_2037146,00.html.

6. Peter S. Goodman, "Sony Hack Speaks to Proliferating Threat," *Huff-*

ington Post, May 9, 2011, http://www.huffingtonpost.com/2011/05/09/sony-hackers_n_859164.html.

7. Stockholm International Peace Research Institute, http://www.sipri.org/.

8. "Dubai Company Gives Up on Ports Deal," CBS News, February 11, 2009, http://www.cbsnews.com/stories/2006/03/09/politics/main1385030.shtml.

9. European Commission, Directorate-General for Agriculture and Rural Development, *The Common Agricultural Policy Explained,* http://ec.europa.eu/agriculture/publi/capexplained/cap_en.pdf.

10. "Undervalued Yuan Hurting India's Exports: RBI," *SME Times,* April 2, 2011, http://smetimes.tradeindia.com/smetimes/news/top-stories/2011/Apr/02/undervalued-yuan-hurting-india-exports-rbi35578.html. Carla Simoes, "Weak Yuan as Big a Brazil Worry as Dollar, Rousseff Aide Says," Bloomberg, January 11, 2011, http://www.bloomberg.com/news/2011-01-11/weak-yuan-is-as-big-a-brazil-worry-as-u-s-dollar-aide-to-president-says.html.

11. Barry Eichengreen, *Exorbitant Privilege: The Rise and Fall of the Dollar and the Future of the International Monetary System* (New York: Oxford University Press, 2011), 2.

12. Dan Breznitz and Michael Murphree, "Run of the Red Queen," *China Economic Quarterly* (September 2010): 21–25, http://www.theairnet.org/files/research/breznitz/Run_of_the_Red_Queen_Article.pdf.

13. "China's Indigenous Innovation Policy and U.S. Interests," written testimony of Dr. Philip Levy, resident scholar, American Enterprise Institute, Washington, D.C., before the House Committee on Foreign Affairs, Subcommittee on Terrorism, Nonproliferation, and Trade, March 9, 2011, http://foreignaffairs.house.gov/112/lev030911.pdf.

14. Dieter Ernst, "It's Time for China to Upgrade Standards System," East-West Center, July 19, 2010, http://www.eastwestcenter.org/news-center/east-west-wire/its-time-for-china-to-upgrade-standards-system/.

15. Ibid.

16. "No Exception; Apple 'Must' Install Chinese 'Green Dam Youth Escort' Filtering Software," *International Business Times,* June 12, 2009, http://au.ibtimes.com/articles/20090612/no-exception-apple-039-must-039-install-chinese-039-green-dam-youth-escort-039-filtering-software.htm.

17. Quoted in Ron Deibert and Rafal Rohozinski, "The New Cyber

Military-Industrial Complex," *Globe and Mail,* March 28, 2011, http://www.theglobeandmail.com/news/opinions/opinion/the-new-cyber-military-industrial-complex/article1957159/.

18. David Bosco, "A Looming Turf War over Internet Governance?," *Foreign Policy,* August 17, 2011, http://bosco.foreignpolicy.com/posts/2011/08/17/a_looming_turf_war_over_internet_governance.

19. *Schott's Vocab,* "Splinternet," *New York Times,* February 9, 2010, http://schott.blogs.nytimes.com/2010/02/09/splinternet/.

20. Christopher Rhoads and Farnaz Fassihi, "Iran Vows to Unplug Internet," *Wall Street Journal,* May 28, 2011, http://online.wsj.com/article/SB10001424052748704889404576277391449002016.html.

21. "Russia, Citing Changing Needs, Ends Its Ties with Peace Corps," *New York Times,* December 28, 2002, http://www.nytimes.com/2002/12/28/world/russia-citing-changing-needs-ends-its-tie-with-peace-corps.html.

22. "Statistics," Facebook, http://www.facebook.com/press/info.php?statistics.

23. Clive Hamilton, *The Ethical Foundations of Climate Engineering,* July 2011, http://www.clivehamilton.net.au/cms/media/ethical_foundations_of_climate_engineering.pdf.

24. Cleo Paskal, *Global Warring: How Environmental, Economic, and Political Crises Will Redraw the World Map* (New York: Palgrave Macmillan, 2010).

25. "The Arctic Is Poised to Be Oil's Final Frontier," *Seeking Alpha,* September 28, 2011, http://seekingalpha.com/article/296430-the-arctic-is-poised-to-be-oil-s-final-frontier.

26. Fred Weir, "Russia's Arctic 'Sea Grab,'" *Christian Science Monitor,* August 14, 2011, http://www.csmonitor.com/World/Global-Issues/2011/0814/Russia-s-Arctic-sea-grab.

27. Paul Koring, "Arctic Treaty Leaves Much Undecided," *Globe and Mail,* May 12, 2011, http://www.theglobeandmail.com/news/world/americas/arctic-treaty-leaves-much-undecided/article2017510/.

28. Ian Bremmer, "Agflation: The Political Risk Implications of Rising Global Food Prices," Terra Firma, May 2008, http://www.terrafirma.com/Alternative-perspective-page/articles/128.html.

29. Whitney McFerron and Jeff Wilson, "Corn Stocks Plunging to 1974

Low as China Adds Brazil-Sized Crop to Demand," Bloomberg, June 20, 2011, http://www.bloomberg.com/news/2011-06-19/record-corn-harvests-can-t-meet-world-demand.html.

30. Ira Matuschke, "Rapid Urbanization and Food Security: Using Food Density Maps to Identify Future Food Security Hotspots," Food and Agriculture Organization, contributed paper prepared for presentation at the International Association of Agricultural Economists Conference, Beijing, China, August 16–22, 2009.

31. Richard Dobbs and Shirish Sankhe, "Comparing Urbanization in China and India," *McKinsey Quarterly,* July 2010.

32. Ambrose Evans-Pritchard, "The Backlash Begins against the World Landgrab," *Telegraph,* September 12, 2010, http://www.telegraph.co.uk/finance/comment/ambroseevans_pritchard/7997910/The-backlash-begins-against-the-world-landgrab.html.

33. Lester R. Brown, "The New Geopolitics of Food," *Foreign Policy,* May/June 2011, http://www.foreignpolicy.com/articles/2011/04/25/the_new_geopolitics_of_food?page=full.

34. OECD/Food and Agriculture Organization of the United Nations (2011), *OECD-FAO Agricultural Outlook 2011–2020,* OECD Publishing, http://www.oecd-ilibrary.org/agriculture-and-food/oecd-fao-agricultural-outlook-2011_agr_outlook-2011-en.

35. Intergovernmental Panel on Climate Change, "Climate Change 2007: Synthesis Report," http://www.ipcc.ch/publications_and_data/ar4/syr/en/mains1.html.

36. Javier Blas, "Nations Make Secret Deals over Grain," *Financial Times,* April 10, 2008, http://www.ft.com/intl/cms/s/0/c4cb03dc-074a-11dd-b41e-0000779fd2ac.html#axzz1bFTh1klM.

37. Brown, "The New Geopolitics of Food."

38. Tom Burgis, "Madagascar Scraps Daewoo Farm Deal," *Financial Times,* March 18, 2009, http://www.ft.com/intl/cms/s/0/7e133310-13ba-11de-9e32-0000779fd2ac.html#axzz1RujI3Erx.

39. Derrick McElheron, "Why Is 'Food Security' Sparking Unrest?," CNN.com, September 24, 2010, http://edition.cnn.com/2010/BUSINESS/09/22/un.food.security.poverty/index.html.

40. National Association of Conservation Districts website: Water Education Resources, http://www.nacdnet.org/education/resources/water/.

41. Aaron Wolf, Annika Kramer, Alexander Carius, and Geoffrey Da-
belko, "Peace in the Pipeline," BBC, February 13, 2009, http://news.bbc
.co.uk/2/hi/science/nature/7886646.stm.

42. "Water Wars: Hydropotential or Hydrohype," *Revolve,* April 15, 2011,
http://www.revolve-magazine.com/2011/04/15/water-wars/. Annan said,
"Fierce competition for freshwater may well become a source of conflict
and wars in the future."

43. "A Handbook for Integrated Water Resources Management in Basins,"
Global Water Partnership, 2009, http://www.unwater.org/downloads/
gwp_inbo%20handbook%20for%20iwrm%20in%20basins_eng.pdf.

44. Ken Conca, Joanne Neukirchen, and Fengshi Wu, "Is There a Global
Rivers Regime?," The Harrison Program on the Future Global Agenda,
2003.

45. Lenntech Water Treatment Solutions, "Use of Water in Food and Agriculture," http://www.lenntech.com/water-food-agriculture.htm#ixzz1
QbUneTaN.

46. Brahma Chellaney, "A Rising Hydro-Hegemon Raising Worries Downstream," *Japan Times* online, September 21, 2011, http://www.japantimes
.co.jp/text/eo20110921bc.html.

47. Jack Shenker, "Egypt's Nile: Nation Puts Great River at Heart of
Its Security," *Guardian,* June 25, 2010, http://www.guardian.co.uk/
world/2010/jun/25/egypt-nile-security-cut-water-supply.

CHAPTER FOUR: Winners and Losers

1. In fact, the Maldives boasts the lowest highest point of any country, at
about seven and a half feet. CIA World Factbook, "Maldives," https://
www.cia.gov/library/publications/the-world-factbook/geos/mv.html.
"Entire Maldives Cabinet Resigns," Al Jazeera, June 20, 2010, http://
english.aljazeera.net/news/asia/2010/06/201062915490741700.html. "The
Maldives: A Sinking Paradise," *Green Hotelier,* May 20, 2011, http://
www.greenhotelier.org/index.php?option=com_content&view=article&
id=263&Itemid=2.

2. "Maldives Cabinet Makes a Splash," BBC News, October 17, 2009,
http://news.bbc.co.uk/2/hi/8311838.stm.

3. See Jagdish Bhagwati, *In Defense of Globalization* (New York: Oxford

University Press, 2004); Thomas Friedman, *The World Is Flat: A Brief History of the Twenty-First Century* (New York: Farrar, Straus and Giroux, 2005); and Martin Wolf, *Why Globalization Works* (New Haven, CT: Yale University Press, 2004).

4. See Dani Rodrik, *The Globalization Paradox: Democracy and the Future of the World Economy* (New York: Norton, 2011); Michel Chossudovsky, *The Globalization of Poverty and the New World Order,* 2nd ed. (Pincourt, Quebec: Global Research, 2003); and Harold James, *The Creation and Destruction of Value: The Globalization Cycle* (Cambridge, MA: Harvard University Press, 2009).

5. Pierre Razoux, "The New Club of Arab Monarchies," *New York Times,* June 1, 2011, http://www.nytimes.com/2011/06/02/opinion/02ihtedrazoux02.html.

6. Donna Abu-Nasr and Zainab Fattah, "Saudi King Boosts Spending as Protests Sweep Arab World," *Businessweek,* March 18, 2011, http://www.businessweek.com/news/2011-03-18/saudi-king-boosts-spending-as-protests-sweep-arab-world.html.

7. Quoted in Gideon Rachman, "When China Becomes Number One," *Financial Times,* June 6, 2011, http://www.ft.com/intl/cms/s/0/df1be35e-9073-11e0-9227-00144feab49a.html#axzz1guzyaQ23.

8. "Brazil—Jamaica's Best New Friend in Latin America," *Jamaica Observer,* January 5, 2011, http://www.jamaicaobserver.com/editorial/Brazil-Jamaica-s-new-best-friend-in-Latin America_8270569.

9. Luciana Lopez, "Special Report: BRIC Breaking: Brazil's China Syndrome," Reuters, September 24, 2010, http://www.reuters.com/article/2010/09/24/us-brazil-economy-china-idUSTRE68N1YB20100924.

10. And Turkey is vastly increasing its neighborly trade. Between 2001 and 2008, its exports to the Middle East and North Africa multiplied sevenfold to $31 billion. "Looking East and South," *Economist,* October 29, 2009, http://www.economist.com/node/14753776.

11. Mutsa Chironga, Acha Leke, Susan Lund, and Arend van Warmelen, "Cracking the Next Growth Market: Africa," *Harvard Business Review* (May 2011): 117–22, http://hbr.org/product/cracking-the-next-growth-market-africa/an/R1105J-PDF-ENG.

12. Phil Thornton and Matthew Plowright, "U.S. Urges China to Embrace

Global Business Standards," *Emerging Markets,* September 6, 2011, http://www.emergingmarkets.org/Article/2845846/Asia/US-urges-China-to-embrace-global-business-standards.html.

13. Jon Herskovitz, "Debutante S. Africa Adds Political Cement to BRICS," Reuters, April 13, 2011, http://www.reuters.com/article/2011/04/13/brics-safrica-idUSL3E7FD16Z20110413.

14. Chironga et al., "Cracking the Next Growth Market."

15. Unicef, "Viet Nam: Planning and Social Policy," http://www.unicef.org/vietnam/planning_policy.html.

16. Statistics Canada, "International Trade," http://www.statcan.gc.ca/pub/11-402-x/2010000/pdf/international-eng.pdf.

17. Alan Greenblatt, "Brazil Hopes to Add Oil Wealth to Booming Economy," NPR, September 7, 2011, http://www.npr.org/2011/09/07/1 40213865/brazil-hopes-to-add-oil-wealth-to-a-booming-economy.

18. Norihiko Shirouzu, "Train Makers Rail Against China's High-Speed Designs," *Wall Street Journal,* November 17, 2010, http://online.wsj.com/article/SB10001424052748704814204575507353221141616.html.

19. China Water Risk, http://chinawaterrisk.org/.

20. Michael Wines, "China Takes a Loss to Get Ahead in the Business of Fresh Water," *New York Times,* October 25, 2011, http://www.nytimes.com/2011/10/26/world/asia/china-takes-loss-to-get-ahead-in-desalination-industry.htm?_r=1.

21. Global Witness, "The Kimberley Process," http://www.globalwitness.org/campaigns/conflict/conflict-diamonds/kimberley-process.

22. Alex Perry, "Why Zimbabwe's New Diamonds Imperil Global Trade," *Time,* December 5, 2010, http://www.time.com/time/magazine/article/0,9171,2029482,00.html.

23. Godfrey Marawanyika, "Kimberley Grants Zimbabwe Conditional Diamond Sale," Agence France-Presse, June 23, 2011, http://www.google.com/hostednews/afp/article/ALeqM5jgK132xOZpcGmXNkGy4ljAkc aXvQ?docId=CNG.25892882fa578430e8394f0a58ecba37.191.

24. Viola Gienger, "Gates Warns of NATO 'Irrelevance' Due to Europe Defense Cuts," *Businessweek,* June 10, 2011, http://www.businessweek.com/news/2011-06-10/gates-warns-of-nato-irrelevance-due-to-europe-defense-cuts.html.

25. David Jackson, "Gates: NATO Is Risking 'Dismal Failure,'" The Oval, *USA Today*, June 10, 2011.

26. "China's Development Loans Beat World Bank: Report," LiveMint .com, January 18, 2011, http://www.livemint.com/2011/01/18091000/ China8217s-development-loan.html.

27. CIA World Factbook, "Ukraine," https://www.cia.gov/library/ publications/the-world-factbook/geos/up.html.

28. Roman Olearchyk, "Putin Woos Ukraine on Trade Pact," *Financial Times*, April 12, 2011, http://www.ft.com/intl/cms/s/0/04aa018a-654c-11e0-b150-00144feab49a.html#axzz1bplvGkPJ.

29. Craig Whitlock, "Saudis Detail Alleged Libyan Murder Plot," *Washington Post*, March 12, 2005, http://www.washingtonpost.com/wp-dyn/ articles/A28178-2005Mar11.html.

30. Peter Simpson, "China, Libyan Rebels Hold More Talks," Voice of America, June 21, 2011, http://www.voanews.com/english/news/africa/ China-Libyan-Rebels-Hold-More-Talks--124275129.html.

31. "Top Economist: China's Growth Model Unsustainable," Fox Business, December 23, 2010, http://www.foxbusiness.com/markets/2010/12/23/ economist-chinas-growth-model-unsustainable/.

32. "The Long Arm of the State," *Economist*, June 23, 2011, http://www .economist.com/node/18832034.

33. Tong Yanqi and Lei Shaohua, "Large-Scale Mass Incidents in China," East Asian Policy, http://www.cai.nus.edu.sg/Vol2No2_ TongYanqi&LeiShaohua.pdf; and "Wen Pledges to Curb Graft, Income Inequality as Police Head Off Protests," by Bloomberg News, February 28, 2011, http://www.bloomberg.com/news/2011-02-27/china-police-blanket-planned-jasmine-protest-sites-in-beijing-shanghai.html.

34. Davis Lin, Laxman Narasimhan, and Jun He, "Understanding China's Digital Consumers," McKinsey & Company, February 2011, http:// www.mckinsey.com/locations/greaterchina/mckonchina/reports/ understand_china_digital_consumers.pdf.

CHAPTER FIVE: What Comes Next?

1. Fred Bergsten, "Two's Company" (letter to the editor), *Foreign Affairs,* September/October 2009, http://www.foreignaffairs.com/articles/65232/c-fred-bergsten/twos-company.

2. See Niall Ferguson, *The Ascent of Money: A Financial History of the World* (New York: Penguin Press, 2008); and Niall Ferguson and Moritz Schularick, "The End of Chimerica," Working Paper 10-037, Harvard Business School, 2009.

3. Zbigniew Brzezinski, "The Group of Two That Could Change the World," *Financial Times,* January 13, 2009, http://www.ft.com/intl/cms/s/0/d99369b8-e178-11dd-afa0-0000779fd2ac.html#axzz1Ud8FohlM.

4. Wei Zonglei and Fu Yu, "China's Foreign Strategy: Constantly Deepening and Broadening," China Institutes of Contemporary International Relations, http://www.cicir.ac.cn/english/ArticleView.aspx?nid=1924.

5. "US Treasury Report: China 'Not Manipulating Currency,'" *China Daily,* May 30, 2011, http://www.china.org.cn/business/2011-05/30/content_22667460.htm. U.S. Department of the Treasury, Office of International Affairs, *Report to Congress on International Economic and Exchange Rate Policies,* May 27, 2011, http://www.treasury.gov/resource-center/international/exchange-rate-policies/Documents/FX%20Report%20Final%205-27-11.pdf.

6. "Chinese Professor," YouTube, http://www.youtube.com/watch?v=OTSQozWP-rM.

7. "Fight the Debt Limit Extension," YouTube, http://www.youtube.com/watch?v=XFsqkI5gg84.

8. Brent Scowcroft, "Toast by the Honorable Brent Scowcroft, Assistant to the President for National Security Affairs Beijing, December 9, 1989," *New York Review of Books,* http://www.nybooks.com/articles/archives/2011/jun/23/toast-brent-scowcroft-beijing/.

9. Matt Smith, "Clinton Signs China Trade Bill," CNN, October 10, 2000, http://edition.cnn.com/2000/ALLPOLITICS/stories/10/10/clinton.pntr/.

10. "German Cucumber E. Coli Outbreak 'May Last Months,'" BBC News, June 2, 2011, http://www.bbc.co.uk/news/world-europe-13624554.

11. "Mistakes in Handling E. Coli Outbreak Cause Furor," Voice of America, June 7, 2011, http://www.voanews.com/english/news/europe/EU-Proposes-Financial-Aid-to-Farmers-Hit-by-E-Coli-Outbreak-123365728.html.

12. "Red Dragon Rising: The Coming War with China," Board Game Geek, http://boardgamegeek.com/boardgame/31554/red-dragon-rising-the-coming-war-with-china.

13. Ted Galen Carpenter, *America's Coming War with China: A Collision Course over Taiwan* (New York: Palgrave Macmillan, 2005), 9.

14. The GCC called for a "joint currency" as early as its Unified Economic Agreement of 1982 (Article 22). "The Unified Economic Agreement Between the Countries of the Gulf Cooperation Council," http://www.worldtradelaw.net/fta/agreements/gccfta.pdf.

15. Juan Forero, "Rio's Slums Get Another Look amid Economic Development," *Washington Post,* October 6, 2011, http://www.washingtonpost.com/world/americas/rios-slums-get-another-look-amid-economic-development/2011/10/04/gIQAVnKfPL_story.html.

CHAPTER SIX: G-Zero America

1. A 2011 poll found that less than half of Americans (44 percent) believe it is at least somewhat likely that today's youth will have a better life than their parents. Elizabeth Mendes, "In U.S., Optimism About Future for Youth Reaches All-Time Low," Gallup, May 2, 2011, http://www.gallup.com/poll/147350/optimism-future-youth-reaches-time-low.aspx.

2. Pew Research Center, "View of Middle East Unchanged by Recent Events," June 10, 2011, http://pewresearch.org/pubs/2020/poll-american-attitudes-foreign-poilcy-middle-east-israel-palestine-obama.

3. Lawrence Korb, "Defense Needs to Play Its Part in the Deficit Debate," *Huffington Post,* July 2, 2011, http://www.huffingtonpost.com/lawrence-korb/defense-needs-to-play-its_b_912753.html.

4. "UN Security Council Resolution 1973 (2011) on Libya—Full Text," *Guardian,* March 17, 2011, http://www.guardian.co.uk/world/2011/mar/17/un-security-council-resolution.

INDEX

Also available from Ian Bremmer

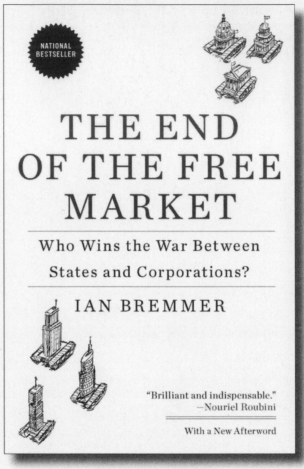

ISBN 978-1-59184-440-2

Now in paperback wherever books are sold.

www.ianbremmer.com

PORTFOLIO
PENGUIN

Portfolio/Penguin
A member of Penguin Group (USA) Inc.
www.penguin.com